Wilhelm Waiblinger in Italy

UNC | COLLEGE OF ARTS AND SCIENCES
Germanic and Slavic Languages and Literatures

From 1949 to 2004, UNC Press and the UNC Department of Germanic & Slavic Languages and Literatures published the UNC Studies in the Germanic Languages and Literatures series. Monographs, anthologies, and critical editions in the series covered an array of topics including medieval and modern literature, theater, linguistics, philology, onomastics, and the history of ideas. Through the generous support of the National Endowment for the Humanities and the Andrew W. Mellon Foundation, books in the series have been reissued in new paperback and open access digital editions. For a complete list of books visit www.uncpress.org.

Wilhelm Waiblinger in Italy

LAWRENCE S. THOMPSON

UNC Studies in the Germanic Languages and Literatures
Number 9

Suggested citation: Thompson, Lawrence S. *Wilhelm Waiblinger in Italy*. Chapel Hill: University of North Carolina Press, 1953. DOI: https:// doi.org/10.5149/9781469658544_Thompson

Library of Congress Cataloging-in-Publication Data
Names: Thompson, Lawrence S.
Title: Wilhelm Waiblinger in Italy / by Lawrence S. Thompson.
Other titles: University of North Carolina Studies in the Germanic
    Languages and Literatures ; no. 9.
Description: Chapel Hill : University of North Carolina Press, [1953]
    Series: University of North Carolina Studies in the Germanic
    Languages and Literatures. | Includes bibliographical references.
Identifiers: LCCN 53062851 | ISBN 978-1-4696-5853-7 (pbk: alk. paper)
    | ISBN 978-1-4696-5854-4 (ebook)
Subjects: Waiblinger, Wilhelm Friedrich, 1804-1830.
Classification: LCC PD25 .N6 NO. 9

To

KENT J. BROWN
(1880-1944)

and

RICHARD JENTE
(1888-1952)

PREFACE

This study of Wilhelm Waiblinger attempts to give him a definitive position as a German author and to examine the importance of Italy as a source of literary inspiration during the early nineteenth century. The most fruitful years of Waiblinger's short life were spent in Italy, and consequently this phase of his career is the most important one. Nevertheless, it is given little attention in the published critical works on Waiblinger. Over and above the significance of Waiblinger's personal experience in Italy, his work is characteristic of many ideas that were current in his day.

Waiblinger left Germany in 1826 and remained in Italy until his death in 1830. During this time he had ample opportunity to travel throughout the peninsula and to become thoroughly acquainted with Italian arts, life, and cultural traditions. There was hardly any aspect of Italy that he did not know and love, for the scope of his interests was as broad as that of any previous German writer in Italy. Waiblinger saw so much in Italy that a detailed classification of his interests has been rather difficult. The chapters dealing with art, literature, and music cover his interest in the humanistic tradition in Italy; those dealing with Italian landscape and people, his interest in Italian life; and those dealing with antiquity, Renaissance, and the Roman Catholic Church, his interest in the great intellectual currents in Italy.

The present study is not an attempt to make a stylistic analysis of Waiblinger's works. Hagenmeyer has already provided a sensitive and elaborate appreciation of Waiblinger's Italian poems. My purpose has been to analyse and classify Waiblinger's comments on various aspects of Italy in the light of literary tradition and of his own creative writing, introducing observations on his style only as a secondary matter.

The advice and constant guidance of the late Richard Jente and the late Kent J. Brown were invaluable to me at the time the investigation was conducted. I am also indebted to A. E. Zucker, who helped to formulate the original plan of the study.

Lexington, Kentucky
January, 1953

TABLE OF CONTENTS

Page

Preface ix

Chapter

  I. Biographical Introduction 1

  II. Waiblinger and Italian Art 13

  III. Waiblinger and Italian Literature and Music 28

  IV. Waiblinger and the Italian Landscape 41

  V. Waiblinger and the Italian People 54

  VI. Waiblinger and Antiquity 71

  VII. Waiblinger and the Renaissance 81

  VIII. Waiblinger and Catholicism 87

  IX. Conclusion 94

Bibliography 99

Indices

  I. Names of Persons 101

  I. Names of Places, Buildings, and Works of Art 104

Wilhelm Waiblinger
in Italy

CHAPTER I

BIOGRAPHICAL INTRODUCTION

Wilhelm Waiblinger has been the subject of relatively few critical works, and most of the interest in him has come from patriotic Swabians and a few bibliophiles who have collected him. There is no good edition of his collected works, and no competent modern editor attempted to establish a definitive text until 1893 when the noted collector Eduard Grisebach edited the poems. Since Grisebach's edition Waiblinger has attracted the attention of only one other scholarly editor, André Fauconnet, who published Waiblinger's *Liebe und Hass*, an early drama, with an introduction as a Paris "thèse complémentaire" in 1913. Waiblinger's other editors have not been as meticulous as Grisebach and Fauconnet. In 1839 a certain "H. v. Canitz" published Waiblinger's works in nine volumes, an edition full of misprints and including among Waiblinger's poems three passages from the first part of *Faust* as well as a long excerpt from Lessing's *Laokoon*.[1] Moreover, this edition is incomplete. Its errors, except for the passages from Goethe and Lessing, also appear in the editions of 1842 and 1859.

In the case of one edition we find an interesting literary problem. In 1844 Eduard Mörike attempted an "edition" of Waiblinger's poems, and he altered the poems to suit his own tastes, by no means parallel with Waiblinger's. He excused himself with the comment, "Gleichwohl ist nichts gewisser, als dass der Verfasser sie bei einer spätern Sammlung . . . vielfach verbessert haben würde."[2] A good example of Mörike's editorial efforts may be seen in the first poem, "Lied der Weihe." Waiblinger wrote:

> Drum hofft der Sänger, auch willkommen
> Mit seinem Herzensgruss zu sein:
> Denn ob ihm schon das Glück genommen
> Was wild und zart, was gross und klein
> Das heisse Herz ihm einst erfreute,
> Der Heimat wie der Liebe Lust;
> Ach, Wonnen, die er nie bereute,
> Die Sehnsucht jeder Menschenbrust . . .[3]

---

1. For information about "H. v. Canitz" see Fränkel, p. 90-95.
2. *Gedichte*, p. v.
3. *Gedichte aus Italien*, I, 8.

Mörike changed it to read:

> Drum hofft willkommen auch der Sänger
> Mit seinem Herzensgruss zu sein:
> Es mische nun sich auch nicht länger
> Verlorner Tage Gram darein;
> Schüchtern verhüllt er selbst der Freude
> Erinn'rung sich und Lieb' und Lust—
> Ach Wonnen, die er nie bereute,
> Die Sehnsucht jeder Menschenbrust.[4]

There is an edition of the *Bilder aus Neapel und Sicilien* and another of *Die Britten in Rom,* but both are out of print. In both, however, the texts are accurate. Less valuable are two editions by Paul Friedrich, one of Waiblinger's essay on Hölderlin and another in the form of a Waiblinger *vademecum.* In the former Friedrich prints an accurate text; but there is a questionable introduction. The latter is a respectable piece of work, but the cover title, *Waiblinger, der Sänger Italiens,* is misleading, since a good deal of the book is devoted to Waiblinger's essay entitled "Aus der Kindheit". The "Nachwort" is valuable for a hitherto unpublished letter to Mörike. *Phaethon* was reprinted in 1920, but the text is inaccurate.

Critics and biographers have not done full justice to Waiblinger. Seventeen years after Waiblinger's death Moritz Rapp published a useful study in the *Tübinger Jahrbuch der Gegenwart* for 1847. Karl Frey recognized the value of this essay in his biography and quoted practically everything of any significance that Rapp had to say. Rapp had known Waiblinger in Tübingen, and he was well acquainted with his friend's writings from the Italian period. His essay consists mainly of personal reminiscences and sensitive critical comment on Waiblinger's early work; but, unfortunately, it is devoted almost exclusively to Waiblinger's German period, and we find relatively little that is pertinent for this study. A half century after Rapp's article appeared Hermann Fischer published an article on Waiblinger in the *Allgemeine deutsche Biographie*; and while this essay is characterized by Fischer's proverbial erudition in matters Swabian, it is factual rather than critical. In 1904 Karl Frey published the definitive biography of Waiblinger in which he exploited all known material on Waiblinger, including letters and the unpublished diary from the Stuttgart period. His work is tedious and has been aptly described by Fauconnet as "détaillé

---

4. *Gedichte,* p. 4.

mais touffu."[5] The next study of any importance is a Tübingen dissertation by Friedrich Glück, *Byronismus bei Waiblinger*, presented in 1920. It is a comparison of the sources, subject matter, and style of *Childe Harold* and the *Vier Erzählungen aus der Geschichte des jetzigen Griechenlands*. Two years later Ilse Ruland presented her dissertation, *Wilhelm Waiblinger in seinen Prosawerken*, at Tübingen. This work gives important background material on Waiblinger's prose works, but there are no structural or stylistic analyses. In 1930 Gerhard Hagenmeyer published his *Wilhelm Waiblinger's Gedichte aus Italien*, the most important study that has appeared to date. It is an exhaustive critique of all aspects of Waiblinger's Italian poetry. In the first part Hagenmeyer examines the literary and social background of the period with special reference to Italy; but the major portion of the work is a detailed mechanical analysis of the poems from the standpoints of form, language, rhythm, and structure. He is concerned neither with the picture of Italian life and culture found in these poems nor with the prose writings dealing with Italy.

In addition to the critical material in these editions and studies there have been a number of articles on Waiblinger in minor Swabian journals and newspapers; for the reading of the works of the colorful *enfant terrible* of Swabian letters has provided many a vicarious thrill for Stuttgarters and Tübingers. This sort of biography and criticism has perpetuated many doubtful legends about Waiblinger, for example, the tale that he died of syphilis, which may be traced back through Glück, Goedeke, and Rapp to a letter by Platen.[6] Of the some half-dozen newspaper articles on Waiblinger that have been inspected, all speak of his "zügelloses Leben in Italien" and of his death resulting from the "italienische Krankheit". The popular mind entertains a conception of Waiblinger as a second-rate Byron with all the Englishman's vices and none of his virtues.[7]

With the exception of the work of Grisebach, Hagenmeyer, Frey, and possibly Ruland, the critical studies on Waiblinger are of slight value. The editions are scattered and often in-

---

5. *Liebe und Hass* (1913). The reprint of the text published in 1914 as no. 148 in the series "Deutsche Literaturdenkmale des 18. und 19. Jahrhunderts" does not contain the formidable introduction that appears in the French edition.

6. *Gedichte aus Italien*, II, 203.

7. *E. g.*, Ubell.

accurate. No one has given any considerable attention to the
most important phase of Waiblinger's life, the experience in Italy, and to the significance of Italy for him as a German poet.
Hagenmeyer has suggested this problem, but neither he nor
anyone else has studied Waiblinger's ideas on Italian culture,
ancient and modern, on the people, and on the country itself.
Most of Waiblinger's published writings on Italy appeared in
periodicals and *Taschenbücher*, thus giving him an audience
that makes his rôle as the interpreter of Italy for early nineteenth century Germany all the more important. While we can
find only a few isolated examples of direct influence on later
writers, it is reasonable to assume that his semi-journalistic
work must have made some impression on the popular thinking
of his contemporaries.

A knowledge of Waiblinger's early life in Germany is pertinent for the proper understanding of his Italian experience.
His childhood and youth up to his sixteenth year are of no importance here, since that period of his life contains no more in-
dications of his future career than the childhood of any other
precocious youngster. Heilbronn, Reutlingen, and Urach meant
relatively little to him in comparison with Stuttgart, where he
began attending the *Obergymnasium* in 1820 at the age of six-
teen. There he pursued his studies with reasonable diligence;
but a more important factor in the life of the young man was
his association with the intellectual élite of the city, such men as
Gustav Schwab, the Boisserées, Dannecker, and other writers and
artists. Schwab must have meant a great deal to Waiblinger to
judge from entries in his diary, for the young man speaks continually of the fatherly advice in matters relating to both life
and art that he received from the older poet.[8] At the same time,
however, the spirited young man did not hesitate to speak of
Schwab as "brav" or even "bieder". In any event, however,
Waiblinger was intrigued by the provincial literary society to
which Schwab introduced him in Stuttgart. At this time he
planned several dramas, *Theoderich, Die Maler, Franz von
Sickingen,* and *Liebe und Hass,* but we have only the last.

Liebe und Hass is immature and cannot compare in literary
merit with the work of a more talented seventeen-year-old such
as Hugo von Hofmannsthal. However, it is important for our

---

8. *Werke,* IV, 340 *et seq.*

purpose in that it is set in Italy and represents the young author's early conception of his future home. At this time Waiblinger was infected with an even wilder idea of Italian life than that reflected in *Fiesco* or Vulpius' *Rinaldo Rinaldini*. The Italy of *Liebe und Hass* is more similar to the land depicted by Monk Lewis in his most extravagant moments. Beautiful countesses, dashing marchesi, intrigue, lust, and murder are the background of a poor treatment of the *Romeo and Juliet* theme.

In 1822 Waiblinger entered the Protestant seminary at Tübingen, a classmate of Eduard Mörike, whom he had known in Stuttgart, and Ludwig Bauer. More important, however, was his association with the mad Hölderlin, whose works inspired him to look again to southern lands for settings. In Tübingen Waiblinger produced two books with a Greek background, the novel *Phaethon* and the very short cycle of poems, the *Lieder der Griechen*. The Greece of *Phaethon* is no more realistic than the Italy of *Liebe und Hass;* but, under the influence of *Hyperion*, it is not quite so exaggerated. In it we find the same pantheistic longing for ancient Greece that characterizes Hölderlin's novel, and the contrast with Germany is brought out sharply. On the other hand, the *Lieder der Griechen* were inspired chiefly by the Greek wars for independence.

In 1823 two important events occurred in Waiblinger's life. In the spring he received a letter from his Stuttgart friend, Theodor Wagner, who was in Rome, and Waiblinger wrote in his diary that he read the letter "mit einem unsäglichen Gefühl".[9] He was so enchanted with Wagner's account of Italy that he started south in the early fall. He travelled over St. Gotthard down to Bellinzona, then to Locarno and over Lago Como to his destination, Milan. All of his hopes were fulfilled here. He was thrilled by the great cathedral, the life of the metropolis, and the art collection of the Brera. It is thoroughly consistent with this experience that he referred to "meine südliche Natur" when he returned to Tübingen.[10]

Toward the end of this year and on through the summer of 1824 Waiblinger went through a moving personal experience, the ultimate outcome of which may have been a primary factor in driving him from Germany to Italy. He met in Tübingen a

9. Frey, p. 106.
10. *Ibid.*, p. 114. Note 11

beautiful Jewess, Julie Michaelis, whose father was a local attorney, and whose brother was a professor in the legal faculty at Tübingen. Despite her frail physical condition, she became his mistress. Waiblinger describes in his diary long hours with her; and it is difficult to agree with Otto Güntter, editor of the *Hausbuch schwäbischer Erzähler,* that Waiblinger's relationship with Julie did not go beyond the platonic stage.[11]   In August 1824, they were discovered by her father, and the old man made Waiblinger swear never to see his daughter again. To forget his troubles Waiblinger set out once more for Italy, this time not with a heart full of hope and expectation, but deeply embittered. Again he went over St. Gotthard to Verona, Venice, and back home through Tirol. While this trip did not make the same powerful impression on him as the first journey, it seems to have crystallized his love for Italy and her culture.

Upon his return to Tübingen in November he discovered that his affair had become common gossip. Professor Michaelis' home burned twice, and his secretary and factotum, a deformed servant named Domeier, was arrested for arson. In an attempt to save himself, Domeier said that he was God's instrument to punish the wicked Jews, alleging that Professor Michaelis lived in incest with Julie, who had already borne him one child and was about to give birth to another, and that Waiblinger had simply been a scape-goat. Domeier's story was clearly a falsehood, but the case dragged through the courts until the end of May, 1825. By that time Waiblinger had become a sort of a pariah. Mörike wrote him a letter chiding him for the affair and declaring that the circumstances made it necessary for him to put an end to their friendship, but the letter was never mailed.[12]

Waiblinger was wild with anger about the whole affair, but he continued to write. He completed *Vier Erzählungen aus der Geschichte des jetzigen Griechenlands* and a novel, *Lord Lilly,* of which, however, nothing is known except that he mentions its composition in his diary and later its total destruction. Neither the *Vier Erzählungen* nor any of Waiblinger's other works had met with any success, but the ambition to win literary fame spurred him on. Completion of his work at the seminary

11. P. 501.
12. Mörike, p. 24-26.

was impossible not only because of the affair with Julie but also because of his state of mind. He turned to his literary friends in Stuttgart to help him find a patron or some respectable sinecure such as that of attaché under Württemberg's minister in London. All such attempts failed, and even less ambitious hopes for a position as a tutor vanished. Finally, in the spring of 1826, through Johann Christoph Haug, editor of the *Schwäbisches Magazin*, Waiblinger secured a verbal agreement from Baron Cotta to finance a trip to Italy in return for contributions to Cotta's various serials. Cotta agreed to pay Waiblinger 2,000 florins at once, but when the latter requested a written contract, Cotta pretended to be insulted and finally gave him only one-tenth of the original amount. Waiblinger felt that even this pittance was enough to start him on his way, and in October 1826 he left his native land forever.

From October 1825 until his departure for Italy he paid little attention to his studies. Indeed, he took every opportunity to get away from Tübingen and visit Stuttgart. Even before his trip to Italy he had written in his diary: "Mein Reich ist nicht von diesem Stift. Darum such' ich auch nicht meinen Lohn in ihm. Die Welt ist mein Reich."[13] In his spare time, when he was not looking for a position, he composed several works, a tragedy, *Anna Boleyn*, which was never performed, and two satires, *Drei Tage in der Unterwelt* and *Olura der Vampyr*. The latter has never been published in full, but the former came out anonymously and enjoyed a considerable degree of success. In it Waiblinger attacks certain pseudo-romantic authors such as Clauren (Karl Gottlieb Samuel Heun), Fouqué, Van der Velde, Karolina Pichler, and Johanna Schopenhauer, who, he argued, lost any claim to art as a result of their "poetische Onanie". As the title indicates, *Drei Tage in der Unterwelt* is fashioned after Dante's *Divine Comedy*. Adolf Müllner has the rôle of Cerberus at the gate of Hades, and Franz Horn is Waiblinger's Virgil. The work shows Waiblinger's intense interest in contemporary literature and a rather good critical sense. Most important is the influence of Dante, which shows that Italy was foremost in Waiblinger's mind during these troubled days.

From the standpoint of intellectual stimulation, Waiblinger's two trips to Italy had been highly satisfactory, and his diary

---

13. *Apud* Frey, p. 132.

contains frequent entries indicating his desire to return as soon as possible.[14] Perhaps the source of his yearning lay even deeper, for Rapp tells us that Waiblinger often referred to himself as "eine nach Norden verirrte südliche Natur." This notion came out in the open when Waiblinger was inspired by reading Hölderlin to describe an idealized Greece in the *Lieder der Griechen, Vier Erzählungen,* and *Phaethon.*

There was also the influence of the age in which Waiblinger lived. The most important names of the day were Schopenhauer, Grabbe, Heine, Platen, Rückert, and Lenau. It is difficult, indeed, practically impossible, to find a formula that describes all of them, but the famous quotation on epigoni from Karl Immermann seems to be the best available common denominator:

> Wir sind, um in einem Wort das ganze Elend auszusprechen, Epigonen und tragen an der Last, die jeder Erb- und Nachgeborenschaft anzukleben pflegt. Die grosse Bewegung im Reiche des Geistes, welche unsere Väter von ihren Hütten und Hüttchen aus unternahmen, hat uns eine Menge von Schätzen zugeführt, welche nun auf allen Markttischen ausliegen.[15]

Neither Waiblinger nor any other contemporary fits this description exactly, but his works do show the influences of his literary ancestors from both classical and romantic generations. Certainly he has all the earmarks of the *zerrissener Uebergangsmensch.* On the other hand, he gradually attained a certain literary perfection in Italy; and, while Immermann's theory may be considered satisfactory for much of his early work, we begin to find in his last years a new synthesis of the classic and the romantic such as Strich describes in the last chapter of his *Klassik und Romantik.*

Another factor in Waiblinger's migration to Italy was the interest shown in that country by earlier German literary men during the preceding half century. In the latter part of the eighteenth century such authors as Goethe, Heine, Karl Philipp Moritz, and Maler Müller had visited Italy and written widely read accounts of the country; and in the early nineteenth century the Schlegels, Madame de Staël, and Chateaubriand travelled in Italy and wrote about the country. Waiblinger knew and read the famous author of *De l'Allemagne,* and he was undoubtedly impressed by *Corinne.*[16] He was acquainted not

---

14. *Ibid.,* p. 117.
15. Cited *apud* Hagenmeyer, p. 21.
16. *Werke,* IV, 218.

only with the numerous translations from the Italian that were produced by the romanticists, but he also had a good knowledge of the literature in the original.

It might bo caid that the ultimate cause for Waiblinger's trip to Italy was the somewhat fortuitous agreement with Baron Cotta, made at a time when he was willing to accept almost any position; but in the last analysis he could hardly have been expected to have accepted the offer so enthusiastically, especially when it was reduced to a tithe, unless he was spiritually prepared to go to Italy. After his first two trips to Italy the country almost became an obsession with him, and he felt toward it much as Hölderlin did toward his imaginary Greece or as Lenau toward the backwoods of North America before his disappointing visit.

Hardly any document is as convincing for Waiblinger's enthusiasm for Italy as the account of his journey. Hastening through Switzerland with a light heart by way of Zürich, Bern, and Geneva, he passed over Mont Cenis and descended at once into Piedmont. At Susa, the first Italian city on his route, he enjoyed the figs and grapes ripening in the Italian sun; and then, passing through Genoa, whose magnificent color contrasts delighted him, he went on into Tuscany. In Pisa he began to understand why Lord Byron could have tarried here so long, for he cried out, "Das ist eine südliche Jugend und Zartheit in diesem Toskana!"[17] Leaving Pisa for "la bella Firenze" he found there the most pleasing city he had seen. In spite of physical discomforts and financial difficulties which had already begun to afflict him, he found that the great galleries of Pitti and Uffizi fully repaid any pains he had taken to come to Italy; and he said that in the Palace of the Uffizi, he, poor boy from Swabia, felt like Thucydides when he first listened to the histories of Herodotus. In Siena he made a pilgrimage to the shrine of some of Raphael's works, and in Montefiascone he sampled the famous "Est, Est" and was as enchanted with it as the legendary German prelate. After passing through Horatian country, Soracte and the Sabine hills, he arrived in Rome; and one would like to add that he might well have passed through the Porta del Popolo with its hospitable inscription, "SALUS INTRANTIBUS!"

In Rome he entered at once into the life of the city, not only

---

17. *Apud* Frey, p. 163.

visiting the show places but also mixing with the people and
participating in the carnivals and other celebrations. Cotta,
however, failed to send funds, and the poet usually found himself financially embarrassed; but he bore his misfortunes with
a good humor, as we see in *Das Abentheuer von der Sohle,* in
which he pokes fun at his miserable existence. The Eternal
City offered too many attractions for him to allow such a trivial
consideration as money to stand in the way. He was determined
to make a thorough and profound acquaintance with the city
that would transcend the superficial knowledge gained by the
young Englishman on his "Grand Tour"; and in his well known
satire, *Die Britten in Rom,* he tells how not to enjoy the glories
of Rome.

During 1827 Waiblinger eked out a miserable existence by
his contributions to newspapers in Germany. This material,
which is gathered in the last two volumes of the collected works
along with similar work from the years 1828 and 1829, deals
with his excursions into the Sabine hills. These little trips
meant much to Waiblinger, for here among the simple country
folk he was able to gain real insight into the national character
and forget his troubles. Early in 1828 his fortunes took a turn
for the better when the Berlin publisher Georg Reimer requested him to edit an Italian *Taschenbuch* for the year 1829.
Waiblinger was to be rewarded handsomely, and he turned to
his task with a full pocket-book and renewed enthusiasm. He
completed it in March, 1828. It contained *Die Britten in Rom,
Lieder des römischen Carnevals,* and two inferior stories, *Das
Blumenfest* and *Die heilige Woche.* The work was published in
a large edition toward the end of 1828.

On his feet financially, Waiblinger acquired a mistress in the
summer of 1828, a woman whom he called Cornacchia and who
seemed to be quite satisfied to live with him without the benefit
of the sacrament. He loved the woman dearly, but she could not
hold him at home, for in September of the same year he took a
strenuous trip to the vicinity of Naples and back. He enjoyed
the winter of 1828-29 in Rome with Cornacchia, who provided
him with a happy domestic life while he pursued his work. In
the spring of 1829 Reimer published a collection of poems,
Blüten der Muse aus Rom, and his tragedy written some four
years earlier, *Anna Boleyn,* and gave him a commission to edit

another *Taschenbuch*. The full title of this almanac was *Taschenbuch aus Italien und Griechenland auf das Jahr 1830*, but it contained nothing about Greece. It was solely the work of the editor except for a romance by August Kopisch, *König Jakob vor Belvedere*. Waiblinger's contributions were *Francesco Spina* and *Das Märchen von der blauen Grotte*, both long narrative works, and *Bilder aus Neapel*, a series of impressions of that city from his journey during the previous fall. Among his other work of this year is an autobiographical sketch drawn from his diary, *Erinnerungen aus der Kindheit*, which his friend Winkler published in his *Dresdner Abendzeitung*. Another work drawn from the diary of his Tübingen years is *Friedrich Hölderlins Leben, Dichtung und Wahnsinn*, an evaluation of the great poet both in sanity and in insanity. This latter was published by Brockhaus in his *Zeitgenossen*. Throughout his stay in Italy Waiblinger sent travel sketches regularly to Cotta's Stuttgart newspapers.

With his literary work for the year complete, Waiblinger left Rome immediately after the installation of Pius VIII in May for an extended southern tour which took him down through Naples and Sicily. Upon his return to Rome in October 1829 he took sick as a result of hardships endured on the trip and died after a lingering illness on 15 January 1830. One of his last acts was to entrust the diary covering the last five years to his friend, Wilhelm Schluttig, a young Saxon philologist; but Schluttig died soon thereafter, and the valuable document was lost. Both Waiblinger and Schluttig are buried in the Cimitero de' Protestanti near the Pyramid of Cestius.

Waiblinger's Italian experience was rich and fruitful. Italy was the fulfillment of his dreams, for here he found the broadest field for his literary activity. He was prolific, but at the same time his work shows constant improvement and promise of future achievement. Italy was in no way a strictly personal matter with him, for he had his task to perform. He had gone to Italy under specific instructions from Cotta to write accounts of his travels for German newspapers, and while he soon broke with Cotta, he did not forget this mission. He wrote for many different papers, contributing travel sketches, tales from Italian life, and poetry inspired by Italian scenes, manners, and customs. From the style of his travel essays it is evident that

he wrote for a wide public, and his work is distinguished by
clarity and objectivity.

In identifying the most important aspects of Italy for
Waiblinger one finds that he has covered nearly all the subject
matter contained in the works of other writers who deal with
Italy. He chose that which seemed to have the broadest appeal,
and under the next seven chapters his broad interests will be
examined in detail.

CHAPTER II

WAIBLINGER AND ITALIAN ART

In the sixteenth and seventeenth centuries Italian art failed to receive the same attention from travellers that it enjoys today. Spon, a minor travel writer in the late seventeenth century, said, "C'est seulement l'amour de l'antiquité qui m'a fait entreprendre le voyage d'Italie et de Grèce,"[1] and he defined antiquity as the literature and history of Greece and Rome. In the eighteenth century up to the time of Rousseau the aristocratic tastes of the age of Louis XIV prevailed, and admiration of the Italian masters was restricted to such painters as the Raphael of the later manner and the Bolognesi, especially Guido Reni. The remains of antiquity which travellers found attracted them principally because of possible associations with Latin authors.

During the middle of the eighteenth century there was a European-wide revolution in art criticism. Winckelmann broke with prevailing tastes in painting and sculpture when he sought to return to the basic principles of great art which he found in the masterpieces of the ancient Greeks; and from the date of the publication of his famous *Gedanken über die Nachahmung der griechischen Werke in der Malerei und Bildhauerkunst* (1754), pseudo-classicism and rococo were on the wane. Exactly ten years later came his monumental *Geschichte der Kunst des Altertums*, and his work not only caught the attention of such leading writers in Germany as Lessing, Herder, and Goethe, but also became known in France and England. From this time on the art of antiquity was examined with a profundity of insight that Renaissance travellers had never displayed, and appreciation of the art of more recent times also reflected changing tastes.

The generation following Winckelmann began to inspect once more the neglected works of modern Italian artists. Such travellers as Adler,[2] Karl Philipp Moritz, and Wilhelm Heinse began to look for something new and distinctive—"romantic" was the word used by the next generation—in Italian art of the early and high Renaissance. In a similar spirit Elector August III

---

1. *Apud* Von Klenze, p. 8.
2. *Ibid.*, p. 46-53.

of Saxony fostered the collection of Italian Renaissance art for the Staatsgalerie in Dresden. When Goethe went to Italy he sought that which was representative in the realm of classic beauty, but his universal interests did not allow him to overlook other possibilities. One passage from the *Italienische Tagebücher* on the legend of the Holy Virgin reads like the work of Wackenroder or Ruskin:

> Es ist ein Gegenstand, vor dem einem die Sinne so schön still stehn, der eine gewisse innerliche Grazie der Dichtung hat, über den man sich so freut und bey dem man so ganz und gar nichts dencken kann; dass er so recht zu einem religiösen Gegenstande die Geissel der Mahler gewesen und Schuld dass die Kunst gesuncken ist, nach dem sie sich kaum erhoben hatte.[3]

With Romanticism there was a rehabilitation of the neglected aspects of Italian art. Wackenroder insisted on the charm and beauty of the simple and unlearned artists like Fra Angelico, and Mme. de Staël had Corinne to plead in favor of the religious masters like Perugino. Many of these critics at the turn of the century even argued that the primitives were superior to the Bolognesi and the Raphael of the second manner (*e. g.*, Friedrich Schlegel).

In the next generation Waiblinger was the foremost interpreter of Italian art. Men like Platen and Heine who had travelled extensively in Italy had hardly touched on the subject. Waiblinger was too late to be included among the first romanticists, yet he was early enough to feel the full impact of both classicism and romanticism.[4] Accordingly, we should expect some kind of a synthesis between the classic and the romantic viewpoints which had saturated the aesthetics of the immediately preceding periods. We may expect no startling new concepts from Waiblinger, but rather a broad and liberal recapitulation of previous ideas.

That Italy is a land peculiarly conducive to the development of talent in plastic art and music has been a prevalent idea since Mme. de Staël and Eichendorff presented to the world the

---

3. *Ibid.*, p. 68-69.
4. Strich defines an absolute polarity between the two styles. It is a natural corollary that the following generation, characterized by Immermann as epigoni, should establish some kind of middle-of-the-road program in the realm of style and thought. Intimately connected with this problem is the well-known *Generationsprinzip* of Wilhelm Dilthey (*cf.* Schumann).

possibilities of romanticism in the southern European countries.[5]
Even if Waiblinger was primarily interested in Italian life and
the Italian landscape, as Hermann Fischer maintained,[6] he
could not avoid a consideration of Italian art, not merely because
of the force of tradition, but also because of the intimate relation
of art with those two aspects of Italy which, according to
Fischer, interested Waiblinger above all else.

It will be noted later that Waiblinger ordinarily revealed good
taste in his discussions of the arts; and this we may set to the
credit of two groups of Waiblinger's associates, each deriving
ultimately from the same school. Toward the beginning of the
last century plastic art in Europe was dominated by Antonio
Canova, an Italian who sought (rather unsuccessfully) to revive
classic Greek sculpture along the lines of the current literary
idealism. His principal disciples were three northern artists,
the Englishman Flaxman, the Dane Thorwaldsen, and the
German Dannecker, and Waiblinger was closely associated with
the latter two. While it is true that the product of these artists
verges on false elegance and insipidity, Waiblinger learned
much from them about the history and theory of art. Waiblinger knew Dannecker in Stuttgart, where the two were thrown
together in the salons of a little group of poets, artists, and
critics, among whom were Matthisson, Haug, the Boisserées,
Schwab, and Ludwig Bauer.[7] He visited Dannecker's studio
regularly during his first semester at the Stuttgart gymnasium,[8]
and he gained considerable insight into the practice of the
sculptor's craft there. Moreover, he was a good friend of the
Boisserées. Sulpiz even wrote to Goethe recommending
Phaethon.[9] Armed with this early training, Waiblinger's
knowledge of art was further strengthened in Rome by his
frequent contacts with Albert von Thorwaldsen and his school.
Although he learned much about art from this group at gather-

---

5. J. P. F. Baldensperger pointed out in his lectures on European
romanticism at Harvard in 1935-36 that late eighteenth century exoticism
is not to be confused with the romanticism of the next generation. When
William Beckford wrote about Portuguese monasteries and Mrs. Radcliffe about Italian castles, they were merely looking for a colorful background; but *Taugenichts* and *Corinne* are efforts to reveal the living
spirit of Italy.

6. P. 64.

7. For a discussion of Waiblinger's relations with these men, especially
Schwab and Dannecker, see *Liebe und Hass* (1913), p. xxxi-lx.

8. Frey, p. 48.

9. Schultz, p. 10-21.

ings in the Café Greco on the Via de' Condotti,[10] his panegyrics on his friends are hyperbolic and lacking in taste. For example, Waiblinger's "Ode an Albert von Thorwaldsen"[11] contains little more than a series of brilliant metaphors on the work of his friend. Nevertheless, we will see that Waiblinger maintained an objective attitude toward the art of other periods, and his enthusiasm for his contemporaries is a fault in the same sense as Goethe's bad taste with respect to the music of his day. It is to Waiblinger's credit that he maintained a consistent modesty in advancing his own opinions. The truth is that Waiblinger's artist friends were better versed in theory than in practice; and if Waiblinger profited from their knowledge, it is excusable that he failed to appreciate their work correctly.

With this background Waiblinger set out to review the art of Italy in his poetry, *Taschenbücher*, and *Reiseskizzen*. Since he discussed in one place or another nearly all the major monuments of Italian art from Roman times down to Canova, and since he showed no great prejudice for or against a particular school or period,[12] it is best to study Waiblinger's criticism of Italian art chronologically.

Waiblinger went to Italy still enthused to some extent by the neo-hellenism acquired from Hölderlin and Byron; and while he gradually lost his interest in the cause of Greek freedom, he never became indifferent to Greek antiquity. Once in Rome he continually visited museums containing the masterpieces of Greek sculpture, and he recorded his reactions in a series of epigrams. One of the most interesting is on the colossi falsely attributed to Phidias and Praxiteles and which had been set up against a Roman background on Monte Cavallo (Piazza del Quirinale):

> Quirinalischer Stolz, Colossen des Monte Cavallo,
>   Wie ihr mir täglich ersteigt, seid mir im Liede gegrüsst!
> Ewiger Jugend Bilder, der Kraft erhabne Gestalten,
>   Blieb euch die Jugend, und blieb's mitten im alternden Rom.
> Ja, ich glaub's, eure Väter sind nicht die griechischen Bildner,
>   Sterbliche nicht, doch der Gott hat euch, der Donnerer,
>   gezeugt.[13]

---

10. Frey, p. 168 *et seq.*
11. *Gedichte aus Italien*, II, 92.
12. *Cf. Werke*, II, 242-246, for an example of Waiblinger's objectivity. Here he satirizes an Englishman who has *read* about Raphael's "Transfigurazione" but fails to understand how the simple piety of a madonna by Fra Giovanni da Fiesole may represent beauty in another style.
13. *Gedichte aus Italien*, II, 49-50.

Here Waiblinger touches upon several of the most characteristic points of Greek sculpture, the youth and strength of the figures and the sublimity of their conception. Likewise he characterized aptly the Venus do Milo, a work discovered barely a half dozen years previously:

> So zum vollendetern Bild durch ein mächtiges Wunder verwandelt,
> Lenkest den irdischen Sinn du auf das Himmlische hin.[14]

In the Apollo de Belvedere he read into the expression of the figure a contrast between classic Greek ideals and the inferiority of modern times:

> Göttlicher Sieger, du zürnst, dein Angesicht flammet von Unmuth?
> Ist's, weil die bessere Welt, weil der Olymp dir entflohn?
> Ach dir nahen die Musen nicht mehr, du zürnst zu gewaltig,
> Ach das verdorbene Geschlecht schirmet Apollo nicht mehr.[15]

In a longer poem of considerable beauty he recalled the Niobe legend while standing before the ancient statue. A passage from it indicates how Waiblinger was inspired by a piece of this sort:

> O so lang' eine Mutter noch heilig ist, und nur Eine
> Mutterbrust noch fürs Kind ihrer Umarmungen glüht;
> Eine Seele noch leidet, und Eine den Schmerz noch der Liebe
> Den unsäglichen fühlt, Eine für andre noch seufzt,
> Eine mit menschlicher Kraft noch gefüllt ist, Eine mit Treue,
> Eine das klopfende Herz liebend dem Tode noch weiht,
> Bleibst du das heiligste rührende Bild; denn es schuf dich die
> Liebe,
> Sanft wie ein Muttergemüth, stark wie Olympische sind.
> Reiche dem Tod nur den Busen, empfange den Pfeil nur und drücke
> Sterbend dein furchtsames Kind schirmend und zärtlich an
> dich.
> Dein erbarmen die Götter sich schon, ja die himmlische Schönheit
> Zaubert ihr süssestes Licht schon auf die Stirne dir hin.
> Kaum noch gewahr' ich den menschlichen Schmerz, dein erhabenes
> Antlitz
> Ist mir verklärt, und du sinkst eben dem Himmel in Arm.[16]

In addition to Greek statuary in Italian museums, Waiblinger displayed much interest in the Greek traditions in Sicily. On this island where Carthaginian, Greek, Roman, Moslem, and Norman ruled successively, the German poet found the countryside studded with the gems of Grecian art. Here he was able to transpose himself perfectly into the spirit of an art conceived in a style completely different from the austerity of the Roman

---

14. *Ibid.*, p. 48.
15. *Ibid.*, p. 50.
16. *Ibid.*, p. 49. It is impossible to tell from the context whether Waiblinger refers to the famous group by Scopas, now in Florence, or to another of the several surviving representations.

forum. In his ode on "Die Tempel von Agrigent" there is a profound understanding for the beauty of the Greek temple:

Glanzreichste Tochter, dor'sche, des Ruhmes voll
Und Goldes, stolz am Ufer des Akragas,
    Am Heerd, dem nährenden der Waffen
        Blut'gen Triumph mit der Lust vertauschend,

Die aus olymp'schem Göttergelage nur
Dem Sterblichen hellen'scher Geburt des Zeus
    Huldgöttinnen ins schöne Leben
        Hauchten, Persephones heil'ger Wohnsitz,

Noch sinn' ich, ob Ortygias Fall, ob nicht
Dein Sturz ein schicksalsschwereres Loos dem Gott
    In zweifelhafter Hand geschwanket,
        Königin, holde, der blum'gen Hügel.[17]

Not merely did the actual structure express a supreme beauty for Waiblinger, but also the Sicilian background offered an incomparable setting:

Dem Berg entsprosst grossblättrig Indiens Frucht
Voll Purpurfeigen, auch die Cypresse ragt,
    Es reift die Goldorang' und lieblich
        Birgt sich im ewigen Grün die Mühle.[18]

When Waiblinger looked on these noble ruins so strongly reminiscent of the luxury of life and art among the ancients, he was affected with a sadness and pessimism rather unusual for his Italian period:

Giganten trugen, mächtigen Arms, die Last
Des Riesenhauses, dass es der Ewigkeit
    Den Dienst des Donnerers bewahre;
        Selbst die Giganten zertrümmert sind sie.[19]

But Agrigentum had made an indelible impression on him with its magnificence, and when he left he wrote, "Girgenti . . . ist mir mit goldener Schrift ins Herz geschrieben."[20]

When we turn to Waiblinger's comments on the remains of ancient Rome, a definite contrast to his attitude towards Greek antiquity becomes apparent. Greek art inspired in him the spirit of individual strength and serenity that are its chief characteristics. In Rome, however, Waiblinger was overwhelmed by a spirit of intense reverence. In the presence of the Pantheon he was awestruck by the grandeur that had survived nearly two thousand years:

O wie mit namenlosem Schauer
Hängt Herz und Auge da an dir,
Und wie voll schwermuthsvoller Trauer,

---

17. *Ibid.*, p. 143.
18. *Ibid.*, p. 141.
19. *Ibid.*, p. 145.
20. *Werke*, IX, 208.

Voll heil'gem Ernst erscheinst du mir,
Du Stolz der Vorwelt und der Ahnen,
Du Riesenkind voll Majestät,
Von Völkerstürmen und Orkanen
Fast zwei Jahrtausende umweht . . . [21]

The men who left these majestic remains are no less imposing
from the historical perspective. The poet felt that the empire-
building Romans were as great in their own way as the more
intellectual Greeks. In "Das Grab der Scipionen" Waiblinger
wrote:

In diesem Sarge ruht der Eroberer
Lukania's: die Seele begrub der Leib
In dem Gestein, und seine Inschrift
　　Trugen die Götter ins ew'ge Buch ein.

Denn Männerkraft stirbt nie: und wenn Helden auch
Geboren sind vom Weibe, sie sterben nicht . . . [22]

Moreover, Waiblinger emphasized, the ancient Romans left a
tradition of noble character as well as of great deeds ("Nicht
Lorbeer, aber Tugend erstrebte sie."[23]). Thus Waiblinger saw
in the visible remains of the ancient Italian peoples all of their
most admirable qualities.

Waiblinger, who came to feel that he was born an Italian
in spirit, was always angered by ignorant foreigners who came
to Italy to find a playground and were unaware of the beauty
of antique ruins. Nothing illustrates this attitude better than
the engraving that appears at the beginning of the second
volume of the collected works. Waiblinger had ordered it to
illustrate the *Taschenbuch aus Italien und Griechenland für
1829*.[24] A young woman and a young man, obviously Anglo-
Saxon by their features, dress, and haughty bearing, dash
through the Forum for a cursory glance at the ruins of ancient
Rome before they return to the whist table. They are too busy
gathering material for a superficial description of the Forum
for friends at home to notice that they have run down two unfortunate Italian hucksters. Waiblinger, on the other hand,
tried to appreciate the ancient ruins in any setting; and at the
same time he viewed the modern surroundings, whether they

---

21. *Gedichte aus Italien*, I, 91.
22. *Ibid.*, II, 17.
23. *Ibid.*, p. 18.
24. A copy of this rare *Taschenbuch* is in the University of Chicago
Library. It contains all the engravings used by "H. v. Canitz" in the
collected works except the engraving in the first volume, a bust of Waiblinger from a bas-relief by Theodor Wagner.

were man, beast, or thing, with a sympathetic eye. In a letter
to Mörike dated 21 January 1826 Waiblinger exclaimed:

> Welch' einen Christentag hab' ich auf dem Palatin des Romulus
> gelebt! Von den Trümmern der Kaiserpaläste aus und dem gold-
> enen Haus des Nero starrt' ich den halben Tag über das Limonien-
> und Myrtengrün und seine unsäglich goldenen Früchte hinab aufs
> römische Forum . . .[25]

The poet, in contrast with the English tourist, spent long days
enjoying the remains of ancient Rome, and modern changes only
enhanced their beauty for him. Unlike Frau Buchholz and the
Englishmen in Rome, Waiblinger looked at everything in the
old city with intelligence and understanding.

Like the preceding generation of romanticists, Waiblinger
attempted to strengthen the effect of the ruins by visiting them
in the moonlight. In the same letter to Mörike he says:

> Im alten Rom ist mir das Colosseum und das Pantheon das
> Höchste, ersteres als riesenhafte, und dieses als durch vollendete
> reine Architektur. Beyde aber lassen sich erst im Mondschein am
> herrlichsten geniessen. Ich mein' ich könne nicht leben, wenn ich
> vor Bettegehn nicht noch einmal das Pantheon ansehe, ich bin
> sogar etwas abergläubisch damit. Seine Schönheit übersteigt
> aber auch alle Vorstellung . . . [26]

Karl Philipp Moritz had been among the first to attempt to make
the reminiscences of past glory more colorful by the addition of
modern scenes. Take for example, his account of a nocturnal
visit to the Forum:

> Nun war der Platz ganz leer; die Geschichte der Vorwelt stieg
> vor meiner Seele empor; aber der Schleier der Nacht verbreitete
> sich über die glänzende Erscheinung; und in der Ferne ertönte
> die Sterbeglocke der Vergangenheit aus dem dumpfen Kloster.[27]

In the first decade of the nineteenth century the cult of *Mondro-
mantik* flourished with such men as Novalis and Fouqué, and
Eichendorff was able to exploit it effectively in Italy.

In this connection it is interesting to point out Waiblinger's
concept of *Ruinenromantik*. In most poetry of this genre we
find the poet conjuring up an image of mediaeval grandeur,
often with a nostalgic longing, and usually ending with some
reflection on the transitory nature of earthly things.[28] Waiblinger did not write about Rhenish castles, but he did use this
same technique in describing the ruins of Greek and Roman
antiquity in verse and in prose. Such a poem is "Die Tempel

---

25. Friedrich, p. 399.
26. *Ibid.*, p. 400.
27. *Apud* Von Klenze, p. 47-48.
28. *E. g.*, Eichendorff's "Da steht eine Burg überm Tale" and Heine's
"Steiget auf, ihr alten Träume!"

von Agrigent". The poet envisioned a pagan ceremony and procession:

> Und priesterlicher Teppiche Pracht bedeckt
> Und hold verschleiert wandelt in Schüchternheit
>   Der Jungfraun aufgeblühte Jugend
>   Rosen ums Antlitz und Rosen ähnlich . . . [29]

But all that has disappeared, even the mightiest have fallen:

> Seitdem mich solche Trümmer umstarrt, seitdem
> Zernichtet mich ein ganzer Olymp umgraust,
>   Der Vater und die Kinder alle;
>   Glaub' ich, dass bald von gedrückter Schulter
>
> Die Welt dem grossen Träger entsinkt, und bald
> All unsres Lebens Mutter Natur der Macht,
>   Der dunkeln, unterliegt, die endlich
>   Selbst sich zerstört im zerstörten Weltall.[30]

The eternally compelling beauty of Greek and Roman architecture, even in a state of decay, had the same effect on Waiblinger as mediaeval ruins had on his contemporaries in Germany.

Waiblinger also inherited the respect of the previous generation for mediaeval culture. One couplet from a series of epigrams on Fra Giovanni da Fiesole might serve to illustrate Waiblinger's attitude toward mediaeval Italian art:

> Dir ist die Kunst ein Gebet, worin du die liebende Seele
>   Immer nach Gottes Thron, immer zum Himmel erhebst.[31]

In his restless life Waiblinger missed that feeling of piety and devotion to God which is so characteristic of the simple beauty of Italian painting before Raphael. In a poem on Syracuse he stopped for a moment in the midst of his enthusiasm for Greek ruins to refresh himself with a quiet walk in "Des Klosters stiller Garten und Blumenweg",[32] and he expressed himself in language contrasting sharply with that of the preceding stanzas on the violent deeds of the Greek tyrants and Roman conquerors. Waiblinger has found some kind of a retreat here from the blinding majesty of ancient ruins and the brilliance of the Italian Renaissance.

Other aspects of mediaeval culture were equally intriguing to Waiblinger. He was especially interested in Sicily, virtually a *terra incognita* until the end of the eighteenth century,[33] and its mediaeval monuments were still little known even in the early

---

29. *Gedichte aus Italien*, II, 143.
30. *Ibid.*, p. 145.
31. *Ibid.*, p. 50.
32. *Ibid.*, p. 140.
33. Von Klenze, Chap. IV ("Sicily").

nineteenth century. In a poem on Palermo Waiblinger lists the
great monuments of mediaeval architecture in Sicily:

> Aber warm von Palermo du schweigst? Normännischer
>   Baukunst,
> Gothischer Kirchen ist dort, maur'scher Paläste so viel.
> Denke des Domes nur in Monreale, des alten,
>   Frommer Mosaik, des Styls der nur gerecht ist vor Gott.[34]

Before Waiblinger's day Sicily had been explored by Winckelmann in his quest for Greek art and for the same purpose by
Goethe. The latter explored everything that Sicily had to offer
the traveller, whether geology, history, architecture, or folklore.
Goethe noted evidence of mediaeval civilization wherever he
found it; but his classical orientation during his Italian period
kept him from enjoying the full extent of the beauty of the
cathedral of Monreale or the Islamic monuments.[35] Again the
romanticists were so preoccupied with their search for southern
color that they sometimes failed to do full justice to the imposing
remains of Greek and Roman civilization. It remained for
Waiblinger and his generation to consider both antiquity and
the middle ages in all their ramifications through the long span
of Sicilian history.

As a good Swabian Waiblinger could not fail to include some
notes on the Hohenstaufen emperors in Italy. The subject had
fascinated Waiblinger, and in his early youth he had planned to
compose a series of fifteen dramas, almost as extensive as Ernst
Raupach's work.[36] This dream never materialized, but when
Waiblinger arrived in Sicily we find him composing an ode in
the form of a panegyric entitled "Kaiser Friedrichs des Zweiten
Sarg."[37] Here, with a background as mediaeval as Walther's
"Ich saz ûf eime steine," Waiblinger apotheosized the emperor
for his heroic struggles against Innocent III, Gregory IX, and
Innocent IV; and some of the stanzas in this poem are so im-
passioned that they might have been written by one of Waiblinger's own Ghibelline ancestors. What interests us particularly in this poem is that Waiblinger was stirred to patriotism by
visible evidence of the rule of a German emperor in Sicily. The
poet presented a motley array of figures adapted to the Sicilian
scene in which he pointed out how Gothic art is an essential

---

34. *Gedichte aus Italien*, II, 159.
35. Von Klenze, p. 114, note 1.
36. Frey, p. 130, 132, *et passim*.
37. *Gedichte aus Italien*, II, 146-148.

part of the Sicilian mosaic. For example, the ode opens with a line recalling the Greeks in Sicily, "So je im Tempel Ernstes und Heiliges . . .," but we soon hear of Friedrich, ". . . des Domes Säulen stürzend . . ." Waiblinger's greatest enthusiasm was reserved for the masters of the Italian Renaissance, the period in which, he believed, the finest aspects of Italian genius were expressed. In a discussion in *Francesco Spina* Waiblinger set up Michelangelo as the representative Italian genius alongside Aeschylus and Shakespeare in their respective nations.[38] In a series of epigrams on Michelangelo[39] the poet used figurative language that expressed for him the collective genius of the Renaissance: "Stürmest, Titanen gleich, du in den Himmel empor," "die gigantische Wahrheit," "ein anatomischer Newton," "dem eigenen Herzen Tyrann."

Waiblinger found the tradition of the Renaissance everywhere in Italy, and he wrote more about the art of this period than about that of any other. Among Waiblinger's most interesting poems are the short epigrams to which reference has just been made, "Kunst und Antike," verses on the most famous artists and works of ancient Greece and the Italian Renaissance. The enthusiasm of these lines expresses the spirit of the age which Waiblinger wanted to describe, and yet Waiblinger was sufficiently discriminating to discover what is characteristic in the work of each artist. Frequently he was able to define the essence of an artist in a couple of lines. Of Titian he wrote:

> Wäre nur sinnliche Wahrheit, und keine höhere, geist'ge,
> Käme Coreggio dir nicht, Raffael selbst dir nicht gleich.[40]

Andrea del Sarto, a long and patient sufferer in matrimonial duress, comes in for two appropriate lines:

> Weil du die Hölle nur fand'st im Weibe, so hat die Madonna
> Dir den Himmel dafür in ihrem Antlitz gezeigt.[41]

Waiblinger found that the artists of the fifteenth and sixteenth centuries gave him precisely what he was looking for in Italy, a *joie de vivre*, but at the same time pride and respect for the worth of the individual. The former characteristic seemed to the poet to be something deeply rooted in Italian character:

> Was für ein Unterschied ist zwischen Römer und Deutscher?
> Jener schafft nicht und lebt, dieser, er lebt nicht und schafft.[42]

---

38. *Werke*, II, 150.
39. *Gedichte aus Italien*, II, p. 54-56.
40. *Ibid.*, p. 56.
41. *Ibid.*
42. *Ibid.*, p. 89.

On the other hand, Waiblinger felt that there was something
peculiar to the Renaissance that other periods of Italian history
have not known.   In the case of Filippo Bruneleschi, the reformer of architecture around the middle of the fifteenth
century, Waiblinger stated that the artist lived in "herrliche
Zeiten, da einst in geselligem Bunde die Künste . . ."[43] Choice
men lived in those days, men whose greatness could not be
matched by the products of the next century when the age of
genius had spent itself in Guido Reni and the other Bolognesi.
In a couplet on Guido's famous "Aurora" Waiblinger wrote:

> Abendröthe der Kunst ist deine Aurora geworden,
> Warum brachte sie nicht neuen unsterblichen Tag?[44]

Waiblinger admired Benvenuto Cellini as one of the finest
products of the Italian Renaissance, a man who was a synthesis
of the most characteristic features of the age. In a short poem
we see how Cellini combined a strong sense of *Diesseitigkeit* with
high aesthetic ideals:

> Gerne bekenn' ich, du bist der Ulyss der Künste, so vielfach
> Trug dich dein guter Humor, Kraft und Genie durch die Welt.
> Längst schon sperrte die Zeit, die schwarze Zauberin Circe
> Deine Genossen im Stall ew'ger Vergessenheit ein,
> Aber durch manche Charybdis erreichtest du endlich die Heimath,
> Deine Penelope schloss dich in die Arme—die Kunst.[45]

Waiblinger's point of view in his discussion of ancient art
was determined chiefly by the extent to which a particular object
reflects the spirit of its age. When we come to the middle ages
there is a romantic longing for the simple life of that period
and for the culture that it represents. Accordingly, when Waiblinger wrote a poetical or a prose description of some masterpiece
from a particular period, we do not find a detailed stylistic
analysis but rather Waiblinger's own reactions to what he conceived to be the spirit of the work. Thus we find him putting
the following words into the mouth of the young artist Eduard
in *Die heilige Woche* when he reflects on the art of the Renaissance:

> Es ist in der That ein schwieriges Unternehmen, in heutigen
> Tagen noch eine heilige Familie zu malen. Es gab eine Zeit, wo
> derlei heilige Stoffe frisch und lebendig aus dem Geist des Volks,
> des allgemeinen Glaubens, der gesammten Religion, aus den Wün-
> schen des Einzelnen, so wie aus den Bedürfnissen des Ganzen
> hervorgingen. So entstanden die ersten Versuche von Cimabue und
> Giotto, so die frommen, gemüthlichen Bilder des wohlmeinenden

---

43. *Ibid.*, p. 51.
44. *Ibid.*, p. 56.
45. *Ibid.*, p. 51.

Fiesole. Es war eine Welt für den tiefen, reinen Sinn Perugino's, für die himmlische Schöpferseele Raffaels, für den hohen Andrea del Sarto. . .[46]

Waiblinger's Renaissance was neither that of Heinse nor that of Goethe, although he had many of the main ideas of both. Heinse, who found in Italy something to stimulate and to satisfy his yearning for titantic emotions,[47] was related to Waiblinger in his extreme enthusiasm and his attempt to incorporate the Italian spirit into his own thinking, but he lacked the philosophic insight of Goethe, whose interest was almost purely historical in many instances.[48] Waiblinger resembles Goethe in trying to interpret the Renaissance without giving himself over completely to the age which inspired him. Today Goethe's intellectual attitude has proven its strength by dominating the thought of most travellers in Italy during the nineteenth and twentieth centuries[49]; but the fusion of this viewpoint with the enthusiasm of Heinse, as we observe it in Waiblinger, has also borne fruit. Among the distinguished travellers in Italy during the latter part of the nineteenth century are Ferdinand Gregorovius, Guy de Maupassant, and Paul Bourget. Each of these men set up criteria by which the Renaissance may be judged, and yet their final concept was always modified by the subjective. Goethe's method of intellectual apprehension was used by all, but in addition we find an active imagination in Gregorovius, a keen and subtle *Stimmung* in Maupassant, and an idea of "feeling" in Bourget. Waiblinger had a notion that the Renaissance was so rich in treasures of art that these masterpieces were well-nigh infinite in scope, thus precluding a strictly intellectual method of perception. His lines on Raphael have a ring of modernity:

Es giebt Seelen, doch wen'ge, die reiner, als andre vom Urquell Sich, vom unendlichen Grund alles Lebend'gen, gelöst.[50]

If the Italian Renaissance was the most glorious period of that country's aesthetic history, then we may properly expect Waiblinger to be less interested in the relatively less important art of the seventeenth and eighteenth centuries. On the other hand, the same urgent need that drove him to seek the *anima* of Renaissance Italy led him to a more tolerant attitude toward the following period. Yet he showed sufficiently good taste to

---

46. *Werke*, V, 21.
47. *Cf.* von Klenze, p. 43.
48. *Ibid.*, p. 81 *et seq.*
49. *Ibid.*, Chap. VIII.
50. *Gedichte aus Italien*, I, 51.

distinguish that which is bad or displeasing. He was far more tolerant toward Guido than the critics of the preceding generation,[51] but he saw Guido's faults clearly. Waiblinger had little use for Caravaggio, who deliberately renounced idealism and sought to return to nature, not beautiful, but brutal and ugly.[52] He praised Guercino in lukewarm terms.[53] Indeed, of all the Bolognesi, only Guido and Guercino attract any attention from Waiblinger; and his attitude reflects the ideas of the romanticists, for whom this group of painters was little more than a nightmare.

We have already observed in another connection that Waiblinger showed poor taste in his high praise of Canova and his school. Otherwise he was silent concerning Italian art in the late eighteenth and early nineteenth centuries. Waiblinger saw clearly that the Renaissance had set a mark which was unequaled in the following two centuries, but he realized that there was a continuing tradition of artistic accomplishment in Italy following the fifteenth and sixteenth centuries just as there had been previous to the Renaissance. All of this he has summarized in a sort of an eclectic canon for the painter and sculptor.[54]

This survey of Waiblinger's attitude toward the art of Italy through eighteen hundred years has revealed much about the man and his generation. He is far removed from those early travellers in Italy such as Montaigne, who looked only for the remains of Roman antiquity, or even from the age of Louis XIV, when men could see no further than Horace's villa or Raphael's *Transfigurazione*. Waiblinger represents the culmination of the gradual process of uncovering the treasures of Italy which had been going on for some two centuries. To be sure, Goethe had been exposed to nearly everything Italy had to offer; but he cherished a bias against the middle ages, and his classical restraint did not permit him to give full expression to the exuberance of the Renaissance, two periods that had to be discovered by the romanticists. Waiblinger effected a synthesis of these different attitudes, and this is the fundamental characteristic of his work.

Waiblinger went to Italy with the firm resolution to explore

---

51. *Werke*, IV, 24.
52. *Werke*, V, 220.
53. *Werke*, IV, 24.
54. *Ibid.* This is a passage in which he appraises all important painters and sculptors in Italy from the primitives to the Bolognesi.

every corner of the land and to delve deeply into its history and culture. Frey has put together from Waiblinger's letters a good account of his first trip to Rome in which we note clearly the young man's enthusiasm for the country he was to make his home.[55] Waiblinger greeted mediaeval Pisa and Florence with no less eagerness than he greeted the Rome of antiquity and Renaissance. The ideal of his youth always hovered before him:

> Staubbedeckte Bücherbände,
> Möge mancher gern drin blättern,
> Aber ohne Mass und Ende
> Will ich, Leben, dich vergöttern.[56]

Waiblinger visited every corner of the land, and he observed the work of all great artists from the unknown architect of the mausoleum of the Scipios down to Canova, all of whom represented and interpreted for him the culture of Italy, uninterrupted for two thousand years. Ordinarily he revealed himself as a fairly well informed critic, but occasionally he tended to exaggeration as the result of excitement or enthusiasm. He always went behind the work to immerse himself in the cultural background of the age that produced it and tried to find some significance for the modern world. His sins of commission outweigh those of omission, for his zeal to see everything sometimes went beyond his ability to comprehend.

---

55. Frey, p. 162-164.
56. *Werke*, VI, 28-29.

CHAPTER III

WAIBLINGER AND ITALIAN LITERATURE AND MUSIC

It is quite natural that Waiblinger's comments on the literature and music of Italy are not as extensive as his treatment of her great works of art. In point of time the twenty-five hundred years of art in Italy represent a much longer period than the relatively brief history of her modern literature and music. Moreover, serious attention was given to the theory and history of art as early as the day of Vitruvius and Pliny, whereas nothing of corresponding significance on music has survived, and the modern literary tradition is quite different from the ancient. On the other hand, the romantic generation had done much to reveal the qualities of Italian poets and musicians just as it had lent a new interpretation to the primitives in art and the religious masters such as Perugino.

The Italian literature of the Renaissance was a fountainhead for the revival of letters in Europe; but, outside of Italy, early Italian literature was almost unknown, and even the literature of the High Renaissance suffered an eclipse in the seventeenth and eighteenth centuries. An eighteenth century traveller like Lalande gave us a quite inadequate picture of Italian literature,[1] and Casanova de Seingalt was totally unappreciative of Dante.[2] Even a man of such fine sensibility as Winckelmann could see no beauty in the Florentine literary tradition.[3] The interest in Italian literature in England has been traced by Marshall, and his results bear out in detail the rather general remarks made by von Klenze with regard to European literature as a whole. Italian literature only gradually secured a firm hold on the minds of English men of letters; and it was not until the time of William Roscoe, who wrote lives of Lorenzo de' Medici (1795) and Leo X (1805), that the appreciation of Italian literature was an accomplished fact in England.[4] Essentially the same chronological development holds for Germany, where, in 1796, Goethe translated Benvenuto Cellini's autobiography for Schill-

1. Von Klenze, p. 27-28.
2. *Mémoires*, II, 142 *et seq.*
3. Von Klenze, p. 38.
4. Marshall, p. 271 *et seq.*

er's *Horen,* the first notable example of German interest in Italian literature since the sixteenth century. Likewise, Goethe showed considerable interest in recent Italian literature with such essays as "Klassiker und Romantiker in Italien, sich heftig bekämpfend" (1818) and "Manzonis Il Conte Carmagnola" (1820). Early in the nineteenth century August Wilhelm Schlegel had translated Dante, and Lord Byron had translated the Francesca and Paolo episode from the *Inferno* and the first canto of Pulci's *Morgante Maggiore.* The new respect for national culture born in the early years of the nineteenth century opened the way for a genuine appreciation of all periods of Italian literature.

Like Italian literature of the High Renaissance, Italian music of the sixteenth and seventeenth centuries is the foundation of much that we call modern in musical technique and taste. Italian operas and Italian prima donnas have remained in fashion all over the world for three hundred years, but it was primarily the writers of the late eighteenth and early nineteenth centuries who gave a distinctive interpretation to Italy as the land of music *par excellence.* In the eighteenth century the English poet Thomas Gray had been the first traveller in Italy to show an appreciation of Italian music as an integral element in the national culture.[5] Some fifty years later in 1795-96 we find an entire novel in which Italian music is a major theme, Heinse's *Hildegard von Hohental.* Madame de Staël's *Corinne* (1807) is especially important for interpreting the Italian attitude toward music in a new light, emphasizing natural ability to compose and sing almost as a national characteristic.

From the time he learned to read Italian, Waiblinger had a broad interest in Italian literature, especially the standard classics. He read Dante and Petrarch daily, and he ranked the former with Shakespeare and Goethe.[6] In an epigram on Dante Waiblinger epitomized his approach to Italian literature:

Alle beten dich an, und keiner versteht dich, die Frage
Ist es nun einzig, was sie thäten, verstünden sie dich.[7]

Waiblinger saw in a nation's literature the master-key to the understanding of its cultural life in the broadest sense. He read not only Dante and Petrarch, but all representative Italian poets, from the middle ages and the Renaissance up to the nineteenth

5. Von Klenze, p. 18, note 2.
6. Friedrich, p. 398 (letter to Mörike).
7. *Gedichte aus Italien,* II, 61.

century, for almost every one of any importance is mentioned and often evaluated by Waiblinger. In literature as in art Waiblinger tried to look at each period impartially rather than to glorify one at the expense of another. Casanova scarcely knew any writers in his own language other than Boccaccio, Machiavelli, and Castiglione, but Waiblinger did full justice to these along with the others. Another important characteristic of Waiblinger's consideration of Italian literature was his interest in mediaeval authors and in the romantic epics, an interest inherited from the preceding generation. The works of Pulci, Boiardo, and Ariosto took on a new charm for the nineteenth century after the revival of interest in the mediaeval themes they treat.

Waiblinger knew and loved the literature of Italy before he visited the country. Before his trip in 1826 he had spent many hours with Dante[8] and had written a satire on pseudo-romanticism in the style of the *Inferno*.[9] Throughout Waiblinger's life Dante was his favorite poet. Sometimes Waiblinger expressed misgivings and fear that he was merely indulging in a temporary enthusiasm for an unduly resurrected poet:

> Sage mir redlich, mein Freund, wie gefällt dir Dante's Comedia?—
> "Ei, ich bin orthodox, halt' an der Mode mich fest."—
> Aber wie so? "Nun ja, das Centrum aller Romantik
> Ist es nach Schlegel, und ich lese die Dichter nach ihm."[10]

However, Waiblinger was quite happy to follow the current fashion after he read the poet and convinced himself of his greatness:

> Hier gilt nur das Commando, man stösst in die stolze Trompete,
> Und als gemeiner Mann folg' ich den andern getrost.[11]

On the other hand, Waiblinger contributed some sound criticism of the great Italian poet. In one passage he described Dante as a good antidote for German sentimentality:

> Möchtest du reine poetische Form, so find' im Homer sie,
> Sophokles zeigt sich, es zeigt selbst sich Anakreon dir.
> Wärest du sentimental nach deutscher Mode, so giebt dir
> Dante nicht viel für dein Herz, aber für deinen Verstand.[12]

In another epigram this contrast between Homer's hellenic clarity and Dante's mediaevalism is expressed in a cosmic figure:

> Bist du gewohnt, mit Homer durch Himmel und Erde zu wandern,

8. Frey, p. 113.
9. *Drei Tage in der Unterwelt* (*Werke*, IV, 115-193).
10. *Gedichte aus Italien*, II, 60.
11. *Ibid.*, p. 61.
12. *Ibid.*, p. 62.

> Suchst du die Klarheit und gern sicheren Boden und Tritt,
> So erscheint dir der Geist Alighieri's, fantastische Wolken
> Tragen im düsteren Sturm dich ins Unendliche hin.[13]

Waiblinger lent intimacy to his remarks on Dante by occasional bits of local color such as a reference to the Sasso di Dante in front of the cathedral at Florence.[14]

Petrarch, the other great poet of mediaeval Italy, also found an appreciative reader in Waiblinger. In one charming little poem devoted to Petrarch, the German poet contrasted the ethereal world of love with the prosaic life of those who would see in the Laura sonnets only a glorification of sensual passion. He who is in love with love finds a favorite in Petrarch:

> Ist dir die Liebe der Faden, woraus das Weltall gesponnen,
>   Der alles Wesen und selbst Gräschen und Sterne verknüpft,
> Dann in Francesco vielleicht hast du den Dichter gefunden,
>   Der das geheime Gespinnst bis an das Ende verfolgt. . . .[15]

But if the reader cannot conceive of this idealized concept of love, then Petrarch's sonnets seem little more than vulgar rimes:

> Oder es langweilt dich: er leiht dir die magische Brille,
>   Aber dein kälterer Sinn siehet zuletzt nur ein Weib.[16]

In connection with Petrarch, Waiblinger made satirical comments on the degeneracy of the sonnet as a literary form in his own day. He felt that the purity of the sonnet had been impaired by literary dilettanti, that the genre had seen its best days in the age of Petrarch:

> Tausende liest man vor in den Akademien am Tiber,
>   Professoren sind es, Monsignori dazu,
> Cavalieri, Grafen, Abbati, Barone, Doktoren,
>   Alle Stände, doch fehlt einzig der Dichter dabei.[17]

Like Dante and Petrarch, Boccaccio had enjoyed a wave of popularity toward the beginning of the nineteenth century, and Waiblinger caught this sentiment with more than the ordinary enthusiasm: "Immer hab' ich ja gern lustige Schwänke gehört. . ."[18] Waiblinger, like Heine, rejoiced in the thought that intellectuals belonged to a higher sphere than Philistines, and on this weak premise he based his appreciation of the great mediaeval story teller:

> . . . Doch über den Alpen versteht man die Spässe
>   Nicht mehr, in Deutschland ist man allzu gebildet und fein.
> Man erröthet, man spricht von Moral, und sie im Munde,

---

13. *Ibid.*, p. 61.
14. *Ibid.*
15. *Ibid.*, p. 62.
16. *Ibid.*
17. *Ibid.*, p. 66.
18. *Ibid.*, p. 63.

>Aber im Herzen ist man, aber im Leben ihr Feind.
>Doch so ist's immer. Man trieb in Eden Alles in Unschuld,
>Und nach dem Sündenfall kam erst der Teufel in Ruf.[19]

Waiblinger greeted the romantic fantasies of Ariosto with
an enthusiasm equal to that which he had for the mediaeval
authors. In the first line of an epigram on *Orlando Furioso* we
are introduced to the magical atmosphere of romance in Ariosto:
"Schwing' auf den Hippogryphen dich auf. . ."[20] And it is this
world of fancy that Waiblinger liked to conjure up for his German
readers:

>Still, mit der alten Mama, der Natur, ihr Gesetz ist vorüber,
>Und von Magiern und Feen, zaubernden Todten und Frau'n,
>Fliegenden Rossen, krystallnen Kastellen und Wundern des Meeres,
>Lanzen und Hörnern und Schild ist sie verlacht und geneckt.[21]

Nor is it this one quality of romance that distinguishes Ariosto,
for Waiblinger felt that he could sing of love as tenderly as
Petrarch:

>Suchst du die brennendste Gluth der Liebe, die Schönheit der Treue,
>Hat Beatrice dir nur Andacht und Schwindel erweckt,
>Ist dir auch Laura's Bild im unendlichen Aether verschwunden,
>Ach, so hast du gewiss mit Bradamanten geweint![22]

In a few prettily turned verses Waiblinger described the dis-
tinguishing quality of Ariosto, the humor that sets him apart
from the naive poets of the middle ages whose unqualified apo-
theosis of their heroes betrays lack of sophistication:

>Dante'n führte Virgil und die überschwängliche Freundin,
>In den Tiefen und Höhn droht dir der Athem zu fliehn,
>Aber der heitre Humor, der begeisterte, wohnte der holden
>Grazie bei, und es kam so Lodovico zur Welt.[23]

Unfortunately, the great tradition of Italian literature in
the late middle ages and in the Renaissance was soon to fade,
and Waiblinger saw clearly how the literature from the latter
part of the sixteenth century on was below the standard set by
the Renaissance. Even the romantic appeal of Torquato Tasso
meant little to Waiblinger.[24] Minor seventeenth century poets
are not mentioned in Waiblinger's works. However he viewed
the rebirth of Italian drama and opera in the eighteenth century in the works of Alfieri, Goldoni, and Metastasio as characteristic of Italian genius.

---

19. *Ibid.*
20. *Ibid.*
21. *Ibid.*
22. *Ibid.*, p. 64.
23. *Ibid.*
24. *Ibid.*

Waiblinger was less enthusiastic for Alfieri than for Goldoni and Metastasio. Alfieri's severity of form groups him with the wave of neo-classical trends in the latter part of the eighteenth century, and Waiblinger felt that this trait set him apart from the more characteristic Italian poets. Thus he tried to imagine a literary synthesis of Shakespeare and Alfieri,[25] and he believed that Alfieri's basic modernity was ill-suited to his classic models:

> Männlich sprichst du, ja selbst der Kothurn ist dir nicht erhaben,
> Noch genug und du streckst gar mit Gewalt noch dich aus.
> Das ist traurig, den Griechen allein nur wäre die Roheit
> Tragischer Sprache Natur, aber der Nachwelt nicht mehr?[26]

On the other hand, Metastasio represents everything that is typically Italian. Waiblinger thought that this poet had the truest and most profound understanding of his native country,[27] and he pointed out that his exquisite use of the Italian language was not only charming in itself but also well suited to the libretto:

> Lieblich bist du, ich lese dich gern, ich höre dich lieber,
> Wenn dich ein römischer Mund, wenn der Gesang dich beseelt.[28]

In connection with Metastasio he contrasted the Italian and German languages:

> Deine Sprach' ist entzückend, ich lausche dem zärtlichen Dichter,
> Aber sprächest du deutsch, fänd' ich den Dichter nicht mehr.[29]

Strangely enough, Waiblinger's enthusiasm did not extend to Apostolo Zeno, the master and the superior of Metastasio.

Goldoni, who revived and remodeled the old *commedia dell' arte*, was highly praised by Waiblinger as a poet who elevated a type of literature as indigenous to modern Italy as the satire was to ancient Rome.[30] His lively Venetian sketches in the local vernacular delighted Waiblinger quite as much as they did the native Venetian Casanova.[31] However, Waiblinger also saw faults in Goldoni, recognizing him as abundantly *freudvoll* but neither *leidvoll* nor *gedankenvoll*:

> So auch wäre Goldoni mir viel, doch Talent und Gedanken
> Seh' ich nun leider im Meer seiner Komödien verschwemmt.[32]

Waiblinger was particularly pleased with the popular theater of Italy. He was always excited by the *burratini* (marionettes), and in a note to one verse he spoke of the large crowds that were likely to watch the ingenious operator put Cassandro and Pul-

---

25. *Ibid.*
26. *Ibid.*
27. *Werke*, VIII, 233.
28. *Gedichte aus Italien*, II, 64.
29. *Ibid.*
30. *Werke*, IX, 213.
31. *Ibid.* and Casanova, *Mémoires*, II, 79.
32. *Gedichte aus Italien*, II, 65.

cinella through their paces.[33] He was equally intrigued by the
San Carlino theater in Naples, a very popular and typically
Neapolitan institution. While this group produced nothing of
permanent value, Waiblinger's essay on it indicates that here
he found something which, in his opinion, was perpetuating a
genuine dramatic tradition in Italy. He wrote that the spectator
should not expect "lauter Stücke von poetischem Werth,"[34] but
he did praise the "Eigenthümlichkeit, Derbheit und Original-
ität der Stücke." The theater poet and manager was a certain
Filippo Cammarano, a man well versed in the tastes of Neapolitan audiences. His plays seem to have been characterized largely
by stock characters from the traditional drama, loose plots with
all manner of intrigue, considerable local color based on an appeal
to local sensibility, and the Neapolitan dialect. Here one might see
Pulcinella, the Buffo Biscogliese, the Buffo Scarola, and the
attrice caratterista carry on in the Neapolitan dialect and revel
in local humor. Waiblinger thought that here in the San Carlino
he had found an indigenous, characteristic drama illustrating
the very essence of Italian life and that this circumstance com-
pensated for the lack of any literary merit in the works of Filippo
Cammarano.

Waiblinger wanted to drive home two points about Italian
literature to his German readers. First, he emphasized that Italy
had a national, characteristic, romantic literature that was comparable to anything that the early romanticists had excavated
for Germany. The Schlegels and their group had pointed out
that Dante and Boccaccio were mediaeval authors without rivals;
and Waiblinger, writing directly from Italy, furnished his readers with the intimate notes that a native critic might have offered. He pronounced Petrarch the greatest of all the love poets, a
poet who sang with an inspiration as compelling as any in the
whole lyrical tradition. After Waiblinger wrote, Ariosto ceased
to be merely a name in the German romantic periodicals and became a poet who added a peculiar quality of genial Italian humor
to his romantic themes. In the second place, Waiblinger sought
everything in Italian literature that sprang from the people. He
was especially pleased to hear a native Roman singing the verses
of Metastasio, and from the extensive works of Goldoni he

---

33. *Ibid.*, p. 89 and 171.
34. *Werke*, IX, 205.

selected the folk pieces as his favorites. In the folk theater he found something that recalled the great tradition of the *commedia dell' arte*. He was coldly distant toward Alfieri's classic tragedies without any native background.

Both tendencies were implied in the search for an *Universalpoesie* by the early romanticists. Waiblinger applied these notions to Italy just as the Grimms had applied them in Germany. Waiblinger was one of the first travellers in Italy to delve into her literature as a means of illuminating her culture and traditions; and in so doing he treated his subject without prejudice and fulfilled his mission of interpreting Italy to Germany. His criticism does not add a great deal to the interpretation of the literature, but his comments are an integral aspect of his efforts to interpret Italy to Germany

* * * * * * * * *

Closely allied with Italian letters, at least for Waiblinger, was the music that he found in Italy. It was neither the delightfully graceful music of the eighteenth century nor even the Italian opera of the period that attracted him. Rather it was the remarkable quality of the Italian language and the talent of the Italian people that allows free improvisation of verse and melody. Of all the great contemporary Italian composers Waiblinger mentioned only Rossini, and his remarks about him were none too complimentary.[35]

We have noted that Heinse and Mme. de Staël, together with the long tradition of itinerant Italian maestros and prima donnas, had given Europe the impression of Italy as the *Urheimat* of music. Waiblinger's special interest lay in the *improvisatori*, and an important factor in directing his attention to these poets and singers was *Corinne*. While there is no statement in his works that he had read Mme. de Staël's novel, he speaks of Rosa Taddei, a well known *improvisatorice*, as "Italiens neue Corinna."[36]

Two points in particular connected literature and this form of art for Waiblinger. In the first place, the *improvisatori* represent a semi-sophisticated folk art; and, as we have noted in connection with Goldoni, Metastasio, and the popular theater, Waiblinger carefully sought in literature whatever bore the mark of the people. He found improvisation cultivated not only in the

35. *Gedichte aus Italien*, II, 85.
36. *Werke*, IV, 218.

fashionable salons of Rome but also in the Sabine hills and in the country around Olevano. Secondly, improvisation consists of verses not only composed by the individual but also sung by him; and therefore Waiblinger saw in the work of the *improvisatori* a genre halfway between literature and music, a conception similar to Wagner's famous ideas on opera and drama. Not only straight lyrical songs but also more complicated types such as sonnets and even tragedies were composed by these talented artists. Waiblinger marvelled especially at the Cavaliere Sgricci, who, at the Roman carnival of 1827, improvised two tragedies on consecutive evenings:

> Sicherlich ist's zum Erstaunen, er improvisirt mir im Fluge
> Wie der Wind so ein Ding, wie 'ne Tragödie, her.
> Jahre studieren andre daran, ein Abend genügt ihm,
> Wie sie an Einem entsteht, so auch vergeht sie an ihm.[37]

Of all the *improvisatori* that Waiblinger met, he was impressed most deeply by Rosa Taddei. One of his most enthusiastic epigrams is dedicated to her:

> Träumt' ich die Muse zu sehn, so lass mir den Wahn! auf Papier nur,
> Doch auf lebendigem Mund sah ich noch nie ein Gedicht.[38]

There are extended remarks about her in an essay entitled "Rosa Taddei" from the year 1828. Waiblinger described her performance in an "academy" of *improvisatori*:

> Es hat jeder, der eine Akademie besucht, das Recht, ein Thema abzugeben. Sind alle beisammen, so werden sie zuerst von einem Geistlichen (!) untersucht, ob ja kein unerlaubtes darunter sey, und unter solche zählte man auch: il Pellegrino. Sodann werden sämmtliche Themen von der Dichterin vorgelesen, und man hat Gelegenheit, zu bemerken, dass mancher im Theater ist, der eben nicht den feinsten Sinn für Poesie hat; gewöhnlich sind es Themen aus der Mythologie, aus der Geschichte, die sich unzähligemal wiederholen, und Dante, Petrarca und Tasso fehlen niemals. Je nach Ton und Inhalt werden sie für dieses oder jenes Versmaass bestimmt, und in eine Kapsel geworfen, sie wird dem Publikum zur Ziehung präsentirt, und gleich nachdem die Themen gezogen werden, beginnet die Improvisatrice die Ausführung... das heftigste Mimenspiel begleitet den Gesang und seinen oft dramatischen Inhalt, und wenn sie zuweilen—doch ist's höchst selten—fehlt und den Vers wiederholen muss, so erinnert uns das nur daran, dass sie thätig, dass sie Dichterin, Schöpferin ist, und nicht bloss vorträgt, was nicht mehr lebendig ist.[39]

It is interesting to observe that Waiblinger emphasized the genius and originality of the poetess as primary qualities. This

---

37. *Gedichte aus Italien*, II, 67.
38. *Ibid.*, p. 66.
39. *Werke*, IV, 199-201.

idea goes back to some of his earliest notions of poetic genius. An entry from his diary reads:

> Dem Dichter, welcher das Wesen seiner Kunst im Mittelpunkt ergriffen hat, erscheint nichts widersprechend und fremd, ihm sind die Räthsel der Natur gelöst, durch die Magic der Phantasie kann er alle Zeitalter und Welten verknüpfen, die Wunder verschwinden und doch verwandelt sich alles in Wunder.[40]

Waiblinger felt that the extemporaneous recitations of this poetess were endowed with "eine hübsche reine Sprache, eine lebendige Phantasie, ein richtiges, edles Gefühl,"[41] and these qualities elevated the simple improvisations of Rosa Taddei to lyrical heights.

Waiblinger constantly brought out the great difference between the Italian and the German. The latter could not possibly perform the feat of a Sgricci in composing a tragedy. Comparing Schiller with Sgricci, he observed:

> Eine Tragödie zu improvisiren, worin gegenwärtig Sgricci von Arezzo der berühmteste ist, das scheint für uns Deutsche anfangs eine Unmöglichkeit. Wir wissen, wie lange Geburtsschmerzen unsere ersten dramatischen Autoren gelitten, wissen, wie lange Schiller seinen Wallenstein in sich trug, wir wissen, welch reifes Studium, welch anhaltende Überlegung die Struktur einer Tragödie nöthig macht, und sprechen darum einem Improvisatore jede Möglichkeit ab, auch nur ein mittelmässiges Werk aus dem Stegreif zu liefern. Aber wir bedenken dabei nicht, wie verschieden eine italienische Tragödie von einer deutschen ist. Nehmen wir den grössten Dramatiker Italiens, Alfieri, zur Hand, so werden wir bald unsere Meinung ändern. Seine Tragödie ist so einfach in der Intrike und in der Anlage, in Akten und Personen, dass es uns denselben Genuss verschafft, ob wir sie vorlesen, oder aufführen hören. Das Personale beschränkt sich auf vier oder fünf Individuen, jeder Aufwand und Pomp der Scenerie ist verbannt, die drei Einheiten sind hier in derHeimath, es fällt nicht einmal der Vorhang, und die ganze Tragödie ist kaum so lang, als ein Akt des Don Carlos. Lesen wir oder sehen wir die Werke Alfieris auf der Bühne, und langweilen uns die unablässigen Declamationen, und die hochtragenden Darstellungen von Affekten, so finden wir's wohl möglich, dass ein Werk der Art an einem Abend entstehen konnte, wenn wir einmal von der Virtuosität des Dichters überzeugt sind; wie wir denn in der That im Jahr 1827 den gefeierten Sgricci auch eine Tragödie hier haben improvisiren hören, die sich noch überdies durch die reine toskanische Sprache auszeichnete.[42]

Even if it is out of the question to conceive of a German improvisation of a tragedy, it is equally difficult to imagine even a German improvisation of verses:

> Aber sie sind mir lieber, denn ihresgleichen in Deutschland,
>   Die man zwar nirgends liest, aber zu Tausenden druckt.[43]

40. *Ibid.*, p. 232.
41. *Ibid.*, p. 201.
42. *Ibid.*, p. 197-189
43. *Gedichte aus Italien*, II, 67.

Just as Mme. de Staël found the *improvisatore* a useful fictional character, so also Waiblinger used *improvisatori* as characters in two of his novels, *Francesco Spina* and *Das Blumenfest*. Francesco Spina, hero of the novel by the same name, and Oda, a quondam bandit chieftain, carry on an improvised conversation in verse at one of the most dramatic points in the story. Waiblinger forgot his own statement about the possibility of improvisation in German and "reproduced" about three pages of this material in German "translation".[44] Elsewhere, he passed over the improvisations of Spina with two sentences merely describing the effect of his song. Waiblinger was equally inconsistent in *Das Blumenfest*, but in one passage he was able to represent in German fairly successfully the manner in which one would imagine that the *improvisatore* Cecco might sing:

> Viel oder wenig
> Was kümmert's mich?
> Bettler und König
> Plagen sich.
> Wem ohne Sorgen
> Für heut und morgen
> Lustig das Leben verstrich,
> Nennt man am Ende noch liederlich.[45]

Very interesting to Waiblinger was his observation that even the most humble social groups in Italy could produce men of high poetic talent, *e.g.*, Cecco, the poor shepherd. Waiblinger wrote:

> Wie sie singen, wie sie die Muse befeuert, wie wüthend
>   Sich im entzündeten Kampf wechselnd beginnen ein Lied:
> Bauern sind es zwar nur, Sackträger und Pizzicarole,
>   Stiefelputzer und solch Lumpengesindel der Stadt.[46]

In a note to these verses Waiblinger wrote:

> Wer hat nicht schon von dem Dichtertalent des gemeinen Volks in Italien gehört? Ich habe anderswo darüber manches mitgetheilt. Im verflossenen Winter brachte ich halbe Nächte im berüchtigten Caffé degli Specchi auf der Piazza Colonna unter der niedrigsten Volksklasse zu, welche sich mit Improvisiren unterhielt, bis man drei oder vier Stunden nach Mitternacht sie forttrieb. Ein Pizzicarol, oder Wurst- und Käsehändler, hatte vor einigen Jahren in Rom einen besonderen Ruf. Scharen von Menschen liefen ihm oft nach, wenn er durch die Stadt ging, und er sang auf allen Plätzen, an allen Ecken.[47]

Waiblinger found the common people improvising in the country

---

44. *Werke*, II, 141-143.
45. *Werke*, III, 106.
46. *Gedichte aus Italien*, II, 67.
47. *Ibid.*, p. 168.

even more than in the city. In Olevano he found a confirmed alcoholic, ironically enough by the name of Michel Angelo, who was especially adept when he had been drinking heavily.[48] The German poet, incidentally, was put to shame by this born poet, whose every sentence could be perfectly scanned.[49] In the summer of 1828, a year after his first visit to Olevano, Waiblinger fell sick there. After exhausting himself with the dull biographies of Nepos and some saints' lives, he turned in desperation to his notes on the folk-song and *improvisatori*. Even the folk-song failed to interest him, but finally he rallied his enthusiasm by copying improvisations for his readers.[50] He included a few *stornelli* (folk epigrams) in these notes, but he turned to the *improvisatori* after preserving this information. He was compelled to satisfy the curiosity of readers whose interest in popular poetry had been excited by *Des Knaben Wunderhorn* and *Alte hoch- und niederdeutsche Volkslieder*; but once this service was dutifully performed, he immediately returned to his favorite theme of the elements of genuine lyricism as revealed by the *improvisatori*.

Waiblinger also found another form of folk music that appealed to him in the *piferari*, pious hill priests who came into the market towns to play their bagpipes and collect alms for needy parishioners. The observant traveller may still find them today in Italian provincial capitals, if he seeks out the shrines devoted to the cult of the Virgin. The engraving at the beginning of the ninth volume of Waiblinger's collected works, originally selected for the *Italienisches Taschenbuch für 1829*, represents a group of *piferari*. Waiblinger's explanatory note is valuable for the insight it gives into his conception of folk-religion and its musical manifestations:

> . . . Niemals fühlte ich mich tiefer in die Märchenwelt versetzt als dann, wenn jene Musik vereint mit den Glocken des nahen Kapuzinerklosters, erweckend in meine Morgenträume tönte, die verhüllten Kapuziner vor meinem Fenster vorüber aus der Kirche zogen und die heroischen Spielleute mit ihren scharfen, aber gutmüthigen Gesichtern, ihren funkelnden Augen, den schlanken, kräftigen Gestalten, in Ziegenfellen gehüllt, von farbigen, malerisch über die Schulter geworfenen Manteln umfaltet, mir ihren Morgengruss entgegenriefen. . .

> Die Piferari bringen ihre Andacht der Mutter Gottes dar, durch Aufbietung aller lieblichen Töne, die ihr gläubiges Gemüth und

---

48. *Werke*, VIII, 243 *et seq.*
49. *Ibid.*, p. 245.
50. *Ibid.*, p. 275-276.

ihre Geschicklichkeit nur zu geben vermag und neu gekräftigt
ziehen sie dann mit heiterem Muthe vom Morgen bis zum Abend
durch die ewige Stadt, um das Herz der Menschen, das leicht beweg-
liche und doch oft so harte, zu erfreuen und zur Spende für den
Genuss zu veranlassen. Wo sie auch weilen, sie können sicher seyn,
stets einen Kreis Hörlustiger um sich zu bilden, und wenn auch
nicht alle zahlen, ärndten sie doch genug für ihre leicht befriedig-
ten Wünsche, um ohne Sorgen hinzuleben, ja nicht selten mit einem
ersparten Sümmchen ihren heimathlichen Bergen wieder entgegen
zu ziehen.[51]

For Waiblinger the music of the *piferari* was parallel to the
paintings of Perugino and Fra Angelico, and this peculiar
Italian religiosity among the common people was something he
admired alongside the great masters of primitive painting.

Waiblinger went a step beyond the romanticists in his study
of folk poetry. True, the Germans of his day were well acquainted with the unsophisticated reciter, but to create ex-
temporaneously was an art that excelled even the skilled recita-
tion of traditional songs. Repeatedly Waiblinger drew the contrast between the German and the Italian with a didactic in-
sistence. He told his German readers that in the south they
could find genuine poetry, genuine music, "den Dichter, welcher
das Wesen seiner Kunst im Mittelpunkt ergriffen hat." The
careful cultivation of some fortuitous gift of nature distinguished Italian folk music, and the living spirit was present.

---

51. *Werke*, IX, i-ii.

Chapter IV

WAIBLINGER AND THE ITALIAN LANDSCAPE

Italia! oh Italia! thou who hast
The fatal gift of beauty.[1]

Such was Byron's enthusiasm for Italy as he passed from
the rolling plains of Lombardy across the rugged Apennines
and down to the sunny fields of Campania. During the middle
ages, however, and up to a half century before his time, travellers in Italy displayed no more of a feeling for the color of
the land "wo die Zitronen blühn, im dunklen Laub die Goldorangen glühn" than they could imitate from the *epitheta
ornantia* of the classical poets. Typical of this early attitude
and in strange contrast to his famous son, Johann Caspar Goethe
was completely obtuse to the natural beauties of Italy in the
900 pages of his tedious *Viaggio per l'Italia fatto nel anno
MDCCXL*.[2] Joseph Addison's sensitiveness to the beauty of
the Alps and the hills of Latium was unusual for his period.[3]
Other travellers showed an occasional appreciation of the landscape, but the first to strike a new note was Georg Christian
Adler, whose *Reisebemerkungen auf einer Reise nach Rom*
appeared in Altona in 1784. He enjoyed the effects of moonlight on natural scenes, spoke of the "Pracht der Verwüstung,"
and described the waterfalls of Tibur as "die romantischste
Aussicht, die man sich vorstellen kann."[4] Still, the tradition of
Watteau's *fêtes champêtres* and the age that produced them continued to influence travellers in their estimation of nature as
she manifests herself in Italy up to the age of romanticism.
Charles Dupaty, whom von Klenze calls the "Rousseau of Italian
travellers," shows Rousseauistic enthusiasm but no real appreciation. Baron J. H. Riedesel, a disciple of Winckelmann, was
likewise quite unable to interpret for his German readers the
natural beauties of Sicily.[5]

Here, as elsewhere, it was Goethe who fashioned the new

1. *Childe Harold*, IV, xlii.
2. See von Klenze, *op. cit.*, p. 20, note 1; the elder Goethe's manuscript
is in the Goethe-Schiller Archiv in Weimar.
3. *Ibid.*, p. 22.
4. *Ibid.*, p. 40 *et seq.*
5. *Ibid.*, p. 60.

style. His *Tagebücher und Briefe aus Italien* and his *Italienische Reise* were internationally famous. Biese speaks in glowing terms of Goethe's development in Italy, of the influence of
the country on his conception of nature:

> . . . sein Naturgefühl wandelt sich von anakreontischem Ge-
> tändel, von Sentimentalität, die in Sturm und Drang heisser Lyrik
> sich austobt, zu gesunder Männlichkeit und Geistesklarheit, die den
> Denker und den Dichter auf die Höhen der Menschlichkeit empor-
> trug und ihn zum Begründer moderner Kultur und zum lebens-
> wahrsten Deuter der Natur nach ihren Weiten und Tiefen
> machte.[6]

Speaking more specifically of Goethe's Italian experience, Biese
writes:

> In dem Mignon-Liede "Kennst du das Land?", dem hohen Liede
> der Sehnsucht, hatte sich schon 1784 die Liebe zum farbenreichen
> Süden und die Plastik der Zeichnung mit einschmeichelndster
> Musik der Worte verbunden. Und als die Erfüllung nahte, als er
> über den Brenner fuhr, da überstrahlte ein langentbehrtes, seliges
> Behagen auch die schönen Landschaften. Aber er legt nicht
> mehr seine Empfindungen in sie hinein—"ich sehe—sagt er—
> neuerdings nur die Sachen und nicht wie sonst bei und mit den
> Sachen."[7]

Goethe's important new ideas about Italy meant much to the
world of literature, and after 1783 we can find very few accounts
of trips to Italy that ignore nature completely. Even if the
next generation did dilute Goethe's plastic imagery with the
subjective, the fact remains that it was highly sensitive to line
and color in Italy.

Chateaubriand looked for the effects of light and shadow
in Italy,[8] and Lamartine was enchanted by the Gulf of Naples.[9]
The opening lines of Novalis' hymn,

> Welcher Lebendige, Sinnbegabte, liebt nicht vor allen Wunder-
> erscheinungen des verbreiteten Raums um ihn das allerfreuliche
> Licht mit seinen Farben, seinen Strahlen und Wogen, seiner
> milden Allgegenwart, als weckender Tag?[10]

were transposed into reality by Karl Blechen (1798-1840),
whose *Landschaft bei Benevent* and *Golf von Spezia* have been
called "kleine Wunder an Licht und Farbe."[11] In German
literature Eichendorff capitalized on the *Mond- und Ruinenromantik* of Italy in *Taugenichts*, and Platen has given us un-
forgettable descriptions of Venice in his sonnets. While these

6. Biese, p. 135.
7. *Ibid.*, p. 148.
8. Von Klenze, p. 90.
9. *Ibid.*, p. 92.
10. "Hymnen an die Nacht," I.
11. Brinckmann, p. 16.

poets and painters were typical of the new feeling for Italian landscape that captured the fancy of the romanticists, the most important figure of the generation for Waiblinger was Byron. The Englishman not only supplied Waiblinger abundantly with ideas and stylistic devices, but he also gave him an abiding feeling for the Italian landscape, as Glück indicates. Accordingly, the two most important influences on Waiblinger in his appreciation of Italy's natural beauty were Goethe and Lord Byron; but much of what Waiblinger wrote about the Italian landscape is original and individualistic, the product of his boundless enthusiasm for the country.

Waiblinger's constantly developing sensitivity to the Italian landscape is reflected in his style. His earliest writing is marked by all the exuberance and exaggerated pantheism of the *Sturm und Drang*.[12] In Italy, however, this ethereal romanticism that turns nature into a sort of Aeolian harp is gradually changed into an objectivity similar to that cultivated by an *Augenmensch* of the Goethean variety.[13] While Waiblinger's life was cut short before he was able to perfect his style and thought, it is significant that he was able to show rapid progress in descriptive techniques. He was able to describe Italy's natural beauties in a lucid and effective style, an essential for successful interpretation of Italy to German readers.

But how, precisely, did the Italian landscape affect Waiblinger? It did inspire a stylistic improvement, but this sprang ultimately from the change he underwent as an individual. The revealing letter to Mörike tells us something about Waiblinger's first impression of Rome:

> ... Es sind nun 7 Wochen, dass ich hier bin, und ich fühle mich auf dem Campo Vaccino zu Hause, wie Du Dich im Garten von Beinhausen. Dennoch aber hab' ich noch nichts weiter als Eindrücke erhalten, und getraue mir nur über Weniges ein Urteil zu: denn das glaube mir, Du magst auch denken und lesen und fühlen über Rom, was Du willst, das ist all' nichts. Ich habe mich seit den frühesten Knabenjahren an nach den sieben Hügeln gesehnt, und ich habe dort keine Vorstellung von all' der Herrlichkeit gehabt. Man wundert sich aber auch, dass ich jetzt schon in den ersten Wochen mich so einheimisch fühle.[14]

Waiblinger developed an immediate affinity for Rome and the whole peninsula. He sought at once the joyous side of Italy.

---

12. See *Phaethon*, p. 213-214, for an example of an immature and undisciplined description of a classical landscape.
13. A passage describing Lago Albano in *Werke*, VIII, 33-34, reveals this change quite clearly.
14. Friedrich, p. 397-398.

He wrote in the spirit of a native, and Rapp described him accurately as "eine nach Norden verirrte südliche Natur."[15]

In general Italy had a softening effect on Waiblinger. His satire lost much of its bitterness. *Drei Tage in der Unterwelt*, an acrid literary polemic from the Tübingen period, is characterized by strong feelings and a bad temper; but *Die Britten in Rom*, much like Julius Stinde's *Buchholzens in Italien*, relies for its effectiveness on a genial humor. The process is obvious in Waiblinger's descriptions of nature when we observe the contrast between the undisciplined imitator of Hölderlin in *Phaethon* and the careful but delighted traveller in Italy. This whole process is brought out clearly in the first stanza of the "Lied der Weihe," one of Waiblinger's first attempts to compose poetry under the inspiration of Italy:

> Ein Sänger, der in weiter Ferne
> Vom deutschen Vaterlande lebt,
> In dessen Geist und Herz so gerne
> Der Heimat Bild herüberschwebt,
> Singt unter Frühlingslaub und Blüte
> Zum ersten Mal voll stiller Ruh
> Im tiefbesänftigten Gemüthe
> Sein Lied euch in den Norden zu.[16]

Waiblinger used imagery from Italian landscape in both prose and poetry. Many of his poems from the Italian period deal with themes taken from the inspiration of historic or picturesque localities in the Italian countryside: "An die Veilchen des Albanersees," "Quelle der Nymphe Egeria in Nemi," "Die Grotte der Diana am Albanersee," "Der Tiber," "Die Felsen der Cyklopen," "Der Berg von Trapani," etc. Waiblinger sings of all the most colorful and famous spots from the Abruzzi on down to Sicily, Tibur, the mountains of Latium, Sorrento, and Capri. The characteristic element in all these poems is a profound and loving appreciation of the Italian landscape, enthusiastic in the Byronic sense and yet tempered with a Horatian strain of refined pleasure. One group of these poems, the "Lieder aus Capri," is of considerable importance, since it is one of the few products of Waiblinger's pen that had a direct effect on other writers. Johannes Prölss has shown in the introduction to his little chrestomathy of *Deutsch-Capri in Kunst, Dichtung und Leben* that Waiblinger's poems on Capri were known and admired by such well known writers

---

15. Rapp, p. 256.
16. *Gedichte aus Italien*, I, 7.

as August Kopisch, Joseph Viktor von Scheffel, Julius Grosse, and Paul Heyse.[17]

Waiblinger generally selected well known localities as the setting of his poems on the Italian landscape. The opening lines of the first of the "Lieder aus Capri" take a typical scene that many a traveller has known on the famous island and suffuse it with an appropriate poetic atmosphere:

> Dem Horizonte nähert sich die Sonne,
> Versinke sie im Meer, in goldnen Bergen,
> Ich fühle stets die reinste Herzenswonne.
>
> Doch welche Lust, wie alle Lüfte schweigen,
> Und die Natur zur Ruhe sich bereitet,
> Den jähen Pfad zum Fels hinanzusteigen.[18]

The image of the setting sun is carried out through five more stanzas, and in the final three lines there is the *interpretatio*:

> So gleich dem holden Wunderspiel der Sonne
> Verharrt nur kurz in ungetrübter Schöne
> Und schwindet bald des Lebens höchste Wonne.[19]

A further illustration of this technique may be seen in the poem "An die Veilchen des Albanersees." The poem opens with a fine expression of the delicate beauty of the humble flower:

> Euch die Frühlingserde: zum erstenmale
> Ihr verborgnes Schmachten bekennend, lächelt
> Sie aus blauen Augen zum Himmel, ihrem
>   Ewig Geliebten.[20]

Then, after several stanzas, the distinctly romantic thought of the transiency of life leads to a consideration of the fall of Rome:

> Und wie selbst die rächende Hand des Schicksals
> Rom auch traf, und furchtbar die Tempel stürzten,
> Wo Triumphatoren den nun gefallnen
>   Göttern die Schätze
> Der besiegten Erde zum Opfer brachten. . .[21]

Waiblinger composed similar odes and elegies dedicated to other famous sites such as the spring of Egeria in Nemi, the sepulcher of the Scipios, Sorrento, and the mountains of Latium. After a description of the scene often characterized by striking poetic

---

17. Prölss, p. 12 *et seq.*, and Ruland, p. 91.
18. *Gedichte aus Italien*, II, 114. Waiblinger frequently showed a preference for Italian verse forms (e. g., *terza rima, siciliano*, the sonnet, the epigram à la Martial) whenever he was not using the Greek meters (mostly alcaic and sapphic, but occasionally asclepiadic) inherited from Hölderlin.
19. *Ibid.*
20. *Ibid.*, p. 12.
21. *Ibid.*, p. 12-13.

imagery, there is usually a reflective element.   An epigram on Tivoli illustrates this method:

> Haine glänzen, es donnern die Stürze des Anio, es stäuben
>   Kaskatellen, es grau'n Tempel und Villen umher.
> Wunder bietet die Vorwelt dir an, und Wunder die Mitwelt,
>   Ueber die schäumende Kluft herrscht die Sibylle noch heut.[22]

In this short poem the first two lines together with the last are strictly descriptive, but the third line contains recollection and reflection.

Frequent among the elements that enter into Waiblinger's nature descriptions are references to the glory of antiquity.   In an epigram on Ariccia[23] Waiblinger was pleased with the cool and healthy atmosphere of the ancient city in contrast with the late unlamented Pontine Marshes, and he recalled the adventurous Sicilians under Archilochus who chose this favored spot as a settlement.   After a charming little note on the Bandusian Fountain and its environs, he added a clever turn referring to Horace: "Trink! noch sprudelt der Quell, aber der Genius fehlt."[24]   The naked mountains and the scrubby pine near Palestrina caused the German poet to utter a sympathetic word about its present sad estate: "Stolzes Präneste, und so schmachtest in Armuth du denn!"[25]

Antiquity is not the only setting for Waiblinger's poems on the Italian landscape.   As he said in the little epigram on Tivoli, "Wunder bietet die Vorwelt dir an, und Wunder die Mitwelt," we find scenes from modern Italy and the life of modern Italians as well as from the ancients.   There is no suggestion of ancient Tusculum in an epigram entitled "Frascati":

> Lorbeer grünt und Cypresse, die Myrthe blüht, die Fontaine
>   Plätschert und rauscht, aus dem Haine glänzet der stolze Palast.
> Alles that die Natur, ein Paradies zu erschaffen. . .[26]

In addition to natural beauty Waiblinger found that the creations of man and even man himself constituted further elements of scenic beauty:

> Gerne bliebst du im Kloster, im Rosengärtchen, das lieblich
>   Wie ein Märchen so hoch über dem Anio hängt.
> Aber ein Frauengeschlecht von vollendeter üppiger Schönheit
>   Zieht aus dem Himmel, es zieht dich auf die Erde zurück.[27]

---

22. *Ibid.*, p. 47.
23. *Ibid.*, p. 45. *Cf.* Horace, *Serm.*, I, v, 1.
24. *Gedichte aus Italien*, II, 47.
25. *Ibid.*
26. *Ibid.*, p. 46.
27. *Ibid.*, p. 47.

He summarized his formula for the program of an ideal tourist in a few lines on his beloved Tivoli. Significantly, it is entitled "Classisches in Tibur," and the content explains the title:

Jagst du dem Classischen nach, und ist's dem Barbaren Entzücken,
  Nun so sieh, wie mich hier Vorwelt und Mitwelt erfreut!
Ueber der Grotte Neptun's wird gezecht, im purpurnen Becher
  Spiegelt sich Tempel und Berg, Hain und Villa Lukulls.[28]

Waiblinger's nature poetry illustrates the traditions of the ancients as well as the moderns. His tribute to Lago Fucino[29] recalls Catullus' tender words dedicated to Sirmio on the Lago di Garda (*Carm.* XXXI), and his ode to the spring of Egeria in Nemi[30] the deep attachment of Horace to his Bandusian Fountain (*Carm.* III, 13). Waiblinger knew the Roman poets well; but, on the other hand, it may have been a common inspiration and a common atmosphere that brought about this similarity. Geikie speaks of this type of affinity in *The Love of Nature among the Romans*:

> A land so varied in its scenery, so benign in its climate, so fertile in its soil, so exuberant in its vegetation, so prolific therefore, in its ministration to the well-being of man, has been feelingly claimed by one of its modern poets to have been dowered with the gifts of beauty. Two thousand years ago the same natural charms existed, and it would have been strange had the Romans proved insensible to them.[31]

Whether Waiblinger imitated the ancients or unconsciously wrote in their manner would require detailed stylistic comparisons, but it is safe to make the generalization that Waiblinger observed Italian scenery in the same calm and comprehensive manner that distinguishes Horace and Goethe's Italian poems. On the other hand, Waiblinger never freed himself completely from the spell of romanticism, as we may see in the following passage from the "Erstes Lied aus Olevano":

Deine Felsen, die zeitgetroffnen, aber,
Mein Olevano, sind's, wo sich der hohe
Düstre Geist der Natur mit ernsten Schauern
Seiner Einsamkeit gerne mir befreundet.
Finstre Wälder des Apennins, in deren
Melancholischen Schluchten über Trümmer
Blitzgespaltenen Wipfeln oft der Wind ein
Lied hinhaucht, das, verwandt mit meinen Leiden,
Meinen Schmerzen, wie wilde Geisterliebe
Mit ertönet, das ich versteh' und kenne. . .[32]

---

28. *Gedichte aus Italien*, I, 41.
29. *Ibid.*
30. *Gedichte aus Italien*, II, 15.
31. Geikie, p. 17.
32. *Gedichte aus Italien*, 1, 44.

But this mood is not permanent, for we hear in "Zweites Lied":

. . . an Quelle
Treuer heil'ger Natur säss' ich, in ihrer
Unerschöpflichen Flut mich täglich badend,
Jeden Flecken vertilgend. . .[33]

The next two songs from Olevano are glorious tributes to Italian sunshine and joy, and an occasional fit of northern melancholy is merely a painful memory of the night before in dark Swabia.

Waiblinger's successful use of Italian landscape in his poems is paralleled in his prose. All of his stories set in Italy and the travel sketches are saturated with pictures of Italian mountains, lakes, forests, and rivers. In the travel sketches a successful description of nature was essential above all else to fulfill the purpose of giving to Germany a complete picture of Italy, for the physical aspects of a country are one of the greatest forces in the formation of national character. In the tales, *Das Blumenfest, Die heilige Woche, Das Märchen von der Blauen Grotte,* and *Francesco Spina,* all of which are set against an Italian background, the rôle of nature is equally important.

In *Die heilige Woche* there is a strange mixture of biographical material taken from Waiblinger's experiences in both Italy and Germany. For example, the German Graf Eduard, the central figure, is modelled on himself and Mörike, and his friend Louis is Ludwig Bauer, the literary friend of both Mörike and Waiblinger at the University of Tübingen.[34] On the other hand, Vighi, the Italian painter, has many characteristics ascribed by Waiblinger in *Das Abenteuer von der Sohle* to the typical Grub Street artist in Rome. The melancholy Graf Eduard is entertained by Vighi's lady friends with a lively *tarantella,* and there is a colorful background for these festivities:

. . . Ein entzückender Blick ist von hier aus das Bild des üppigen, reichen Gianicolo, aus dessen immer grünen, süssen Lufthainen die lieblichsten Klöster, Kirchen und Villen herausschauen, und dessen sanft gezogene Linie ein Paradies von schlanken Pinien krönt. Sodann das alte Rom, über das man frei hinwegblickt, eröffnet über der Fülle der angränzenden Haine, der lichtgrünen Gärten, der schwarzen Cypressen, der reizendsten Lorbeergänge voll Nachtigallen, voll weisser Bilder seine melancholischen, nun in einem Meer von Sonnengold und Duft glühenden Wunder! Dort ersteht die furchtbare Wand des Colosseums, dort liegen die Trümmer von den Thermen des Titus wild umher, dort ragen die Kaiserpaläste grausig aus dem lieblichen Grün vor Evanders Berg hervor; den Friedenstempel bedeckt der Orangengarten, der an ihm hinaufblickt, und hier ganz in der Nähe, in der mannigfaltigsten

33. *Ibid.,* p. 47.
34. Ruland, p. 40.

Gartennatur, neben den dunkeln Hainen der Villa Giustiniani graut
der runde Tempel der Minerva medica![35]

Waiblinger had a highly developed sense for line and color, and
the application of these qualities to his narrative is an unusual
note in early nineteenth century German fiction, for so many
other romanticists depend solely on fantasy for their color.

Das Märchen von der Blauen Grotte is resplendent with nature imagery, since the setting throughout the tale is the picturesque Bay of Naples. One of the most successful passages
in this story is the description of the Blue Grotto itself:

> ... Schön ist eine Mondnacht im Süden, und die Bläue der Lüfte,
> so wie des Wassers ist bezaubernd, aber was sind solche Farben
> gegen das brennende Blau, das diese hohe Felsenhöhle wie mit der
> Kraft einer optischen Magie durchschimmerte, gegen die Klarheit
> des Meeres, das sie mit dem Kristall einer bis auf den tiefsten
> Grund durchsichtigen Fluth anfüllte, gegen die unbeschreibliche
> Helle, die sich wie ein süsses Feuer von ihrem Spiegel aus über
> die seltsam gebildeten Felswände verbreitete, dass auch sie in
> phosphorischen Flammen zu glühen schienen, gegen die Wirkung
> von Nähe und Ferne, von Licht und Schatten, gegen die Lieblichkeit
> des Bildes, das die lautern Wasser von den mannichfaltigen Fels-
> gestalten zurückspiegelten, ja gegen die Schwimmenden selbst, die
> mit entzückender Lichthelle aus dem blauen Zauberbad hervor-
> leuchteten.[36]

Francesco Spina and *Das Blumenfest* are hack-work, and both
stories reflect hasty and thoughtless composition. However,
Waiblinger did not lose his sense for the background of Italian
landscape, and many of the nature descriptions in these stories
are equal to those in the rest of his work. Still, the inspiration
that we find elsewhere is not present here.

In Waiblinger's two most successful pieces of fiction set in
Italy, there are many good nature descriptions. He knew and
loved the country so well that he could paint its natural beauties
in glowing colors. Except for Heine and Goethe, few other
writers about Italy prior to Waiblinger have been able to give
northern European readers an equally vivid picture of the country. Goethe surpassed Waiblinger in the field of geological
observations, and Winckelmann was a more learned student of
the arts; but these closet diversions are not dependent upon a
thorough and loving acquaintance with the whole country that
is so characteristic of Waiblinger. The Swabian's ability to
incorporate this material into his fiction is a step forward in
the appreciation of Italy as a physical entity.

35. *Werke*, IV, 104.
36. *Werke*, III, 25.

Of all Waiblinger's works the stories and the travel sketches were perhaps the most widely read, and the latter were even better known than the former.[37] The travel sketches, printed in the *Taschenbücher* and collected in the eighth and ninth volumes of the works, cover almost all of the best known localities and many of the lesser known ones from the Abruzzi south. Waiblinger travelled in historic territory, but the most important element in these travel essays is his appreciation of the landscape. Some of the titles are even suggestive of this element: "Der Frühling in den Gebirgen Latiums," "Wanderung ins Sabinerland," "Sommerausflug nach Olevano." He travelled on foot and with a donkey constantly from his arrival in Italy up until the time of his death; and according to Frey and Grisebach, Waiblinger died as the result of consumption contracted after the hardships of his journeys.[38]

Some samples of the descriptions in the *Reiseschilderungen* will show the literary quality of this work. Waiblinger rarely indulged in the satire and pleasant small talk that are characteristic of Heine's *Italienische Reise*, for he took the title of his work more seriously and attempted to give his readers a comprehensive picture of Italy. To be sure, he was interested in the people, as we shall see in another connection, but this interest was of quite another type from Heine's, who found company among the fashionable travellers. An account of Civitella's site demonstrates Waiblinger's approach fairly:

> Civitella lag lange schon vor uns auf seinem rippigen, grauen, nackten, wüsten, furchtbaren Berge, und schien kein Dorf, sondern nur ein Haufen übereinandergeworfener Steine. So aber beinahe alle Oerter in diesen wilden Gebirgen; wenn sie nicht gerade auf der Spitze einer Anhöhe hängen und durch einen Thurm sich auszeichnen, so kann man sie oft kaum nach Farbe und Form vom Berge unterscheiden, an den sie angeklebt sind. Auf der andern Seite lachten uns die frischen elisischen Kastanienwälder zu, unter denen der Weg nach Civitella hinaufführt, und bald hatten wir einen Standpunkt oben auf der Höhe der Serpentara gewonnen, wo wir, umgeben von uralten herrlichen Eichen, eine entzückende Aussicht vor uns hatten. Nördlich das grauenweckende Civitella in den Lüften, nordwestlich die vielfachen Abstufungen und Formen des Aequergebirgs, nun, da die Sonne ziemlich hinter ihnen stand, in einem herrlichen Schattentone, über den vielen Olivenhügeln und Wäldern an der Stirne eines Berges St. Vito, oben auf windiger Höhe Kapranica und Tocca di Cavi, ein Oertchen, das kaum ein Adler erschwingen zu können scheint.[39]

37. Ruland, p. 4.
38. Frey, p. 238, and *Gedichte aus Italien*, II, 203-206 (Grisebach's appendix).
39. *Werke*, VIII, 185-186.

In this selection Waiblinger did not attempt to spare the barren, forbidding Apennines, but he was not blind to the natural beauty of the spot.   Just as we have seen in other instances, his land-scapes in prose are filled with the contrast between north and south, Germany and Italy.   In Sorrento he ran into bad weather and made the following comment:

> Wenn uns der Anblick des Piano di Sorrento, diese ungeheuren Orangengärtchen, dieser eigentliche Pomeranzenwald, aus dessen Dunkelgrün hundert lustige Häuser und Höfe hervorschauen, aller-dings einige Worte der Verwunderung abnöthigte, so war es doch natürlich, dass wir uns sogleich wieder über das nordische Un-wetter beklagten, das diese glückseligen Strecken umnachtete und verwüstete.[40]

In connection with this passage it is important to note that Waiblinger always looked for characteristic scenery in the "Land der Citronen und Goldorangen," places that brought out all the brilliance and sunlight traditionally associated with the peninsula.   Such is his description of sunset at Olevano:

> Welch ein göttlicher unvergesslicher Tag! Meine Freunde bese-hen sich die Natur, und ich habe meine besondern Freuden. Wir sa-hen endlich die Sonne hinter den Aequerbergen in blendendem Golde untergehen. Alle unaussprechliche Schöne, Fülle, Klarheit und Süssigkeit Hesperiens lächelte aus den Bergen von Anagni und Segni, wie aus dem Aufenthalte der Seligen, herüber. Daran reichen Worte nicht, und wenn ich Ihnen auch jene tausend und aber taus-end Farbentöne angeben könnte, die in der Landschaft in einander spielten, so gäbe es doch kein Bild von alle dem überschwänglichen Glanze.[41]

He haunted the footsteps of the ancients as we have seen in his poems on the ancient villas at Tivoli, the site of ancient Lavinium where he conjured up visions of Aeneas' landing on Italian soil, and Girgenti where he imagined that he saw a coy nymph hiding behind the pillars of an ancient temple.   His passage on Lavinium is representative:

> Unmittelbar unter dem elysischen Gärtchen gruppirt sich das niedere Cora zum Theil hinab, ihm gegenüber wölbt sich ein wollü-stig rundlicher Berg in sanfter Wellenlinie, und das Silbergrün seiner Oliven bildet einen erquickenden Contrast mit Feigen, Kas-tanien und Vignen. Durch zwei junge Cypressen, welche am Rande des Gärtchens ihr schlankes, dunkles Gewächs emporheben, entfaltet sich, wie in einen Rahmen zusammengezogen, die Ferne, gleich schön durch den Reiz ihrer Farbe, durch die unendliche Weite ihres Raumes, als durch die Mythe, durch die Geschichte, die sie vorzugsweise geheiligt. Denn hier spielt die älteste Fabel Italiens, die sich an die griechische anknüpft, hier ein Stück aus der Odys-see, und die vaterländische Dichtung der Aeneide, hier hebt sich das wundersame blauduftige Vorgebirge der Circe wie ein Zauber-drache aus dem Meere, hier ist der Boden, wo Ulysses gelandet,

---

40. *Werke*, IX, 149.
41. *Ibid.*, p. 103.

hier wo Aeneas, nach der Zerstörung Troja's, vor drei Jahrtausenden Lavinium gegründet. Hier ist die Wiege Roms! Als eine weite heitere Fläche voll saftigen Grüns breiten sich die pontinischen Sümpfe aus, und man gewahrt die Appische Strasse, die nach Parthenope führt: hoch und herrlich erstreckt sich darüber hin die Riesenlinie des Tyrrhenischen Meeres, und die drei Ponzainseln duften mit ihren dämmernden Felsen wie neptunische Wunder aus ihm herüber. . .[42]

In Waiblinger's travel sketches, better than in any other part of his work, his devotion to the physical and the human aspects of Italy is unmistakable. He was able to incorporate this feeling for Italy's scenery into prose essays, poems, and tales. Everywhere some image from Italian landscape appears, for Italy is the fundamental theme of all his mature work. A few previous travellers in Italy had observed and appreciated her natural beauty in parts of their works, but all of Waiblinger's writings are filled with it.

Antiquity and modern times are revealed alike in Waiblinger's work. In Subiaco he faced the dilemma of choosing between a visit to the ancient monastery and enjoying the company of a charming young girl; and, much to the disgust of the latter, he gave up neither and tried to make love to her in the garden of the monastery.[43] This eagerness to see and do everything is typical of his attitude. At times he may describe the pleasing sight of orange groves and vineyards bathed in warm sunshine, and then he falls at once into reveries on the glories of ancient times.[44]

Waiblinger maintained a critical attitude in general, but he rarely failed to exhibit his boundless enthusiasm for everything Italian. He could see little beauty in the rocky and barren slopes of the Apennines, and his displeasure at the filth he saw in Benevento caused him to rechristen the town with the ancient name of Maleventum.[45] On the other hand, a shady nook beside the Lago Albano or a pleasing view from Monte Cavo called forth an appropriate tribute.

It is not unusual that Waiblinger wrote nothing about Italy north of the Abruzzi and Rome, for the most important historic and scenic localities are in the southern part of the peninsula. The rocky coast of Liguria and Lombardy offer entirely different opportunities from the Bay of Naples, Rome and her environs,

42. *Ibid.*, p. 112-113.
43. *Ibid.*, p. 87.
44. *Ibid.*, p. 199-200.
45. *Ibid.*, p. 234.

Syracuse, or Girgenti. Waiblinger, who was liable to go to excess at times even in his later period, did not attempt the impossible task of surveying Italy as a totality; rather, he selected the most characteristic scenes and tried to omit nothing of importance.

At the beginning of this chapter we noticed the development in Waiblinger's ability to record his appreciation of nature. While these comments are still valid, we are now in a position to expand them. None of the excerpts quoted in this chapter show absolute stylistic perfection. Indeed, there are some rather shabby spots in them. Still the improvement over the early writings is obvious, and even more important, Waiblinger at last found a central theme for his creative work.

CHAPTER V

WAIBLINGER AND THE ITALIAN PEOPLE

In this chapter we come to one of the most productive aspects of Waiblinger's Italian experience. Whether or not he exercised any direct influence in orienting the modern tourist toward the Italian people, we find that von Klenze records no previous traveller who made such extensive tours through the cities and the country and who delved into the life and customs of individuals and groups as thoroughly as Waiblinger. The German poet would tarry on the Molo in Naples to hear a public reading of Ariosto by a disabled sailor, he would haunt the lowest and rowdiest taverns of Rome to follow some locally famous *improvisatore*, he would pause in Genzano to take a second look at the pretty face and buxom figure of a village beauty, and, like Horace, lost sleep when she failed to keep a rendezvous (*Serm.* I, v, 82-85).

Earlier travellers in Italy had paid little attention to the people. Indeed, we find not merely indifference, but indignant commentaries on the lack of sanitation.[1] Montaigne, to be sure, had shown a strong interest in people during his Italian sojourn; but he was a Renaissance philosopher who sought universal human traits rather than peculiar national or local characteristics. In short, Italians were scorned by visitors as the unworthy and degenerate heirs of the great traditions of antiquity and Renaissance.

Goethe was far more tolerant of the people than earlier travellers. His essays on "Das römische Carneval" and "Die Tarantella" show a genuine interest in the festive aspects of the land he learned to love, and the little article entitled "Frauenrollen auf dem römischen Theater durch Männer gespielt" illustrates his preoccupation with indigenous art. Still, Goethe was too much of a classicist, too much a lover of antiquity, too aristocratic to seek out friends among the people and acquaint himself with their daily life and customs. Even his Faustine was hardly representative of Italian womanhood, for she was rather the incarnation of southern life in general that Goethe was so

---

1. English travellers on the "grand tour" were especially guilty. (Steinitzer, p. 25).

eager to know. Waiblinger, on the contrary, would see in a village girl of Olevano the characteristic Italian beauty.

It remained for the romanticists to exploit popular color and tradition, and this task was nobly executed in Italy. Arnim, Brentano, Philipp Otto Runge, Görres, and, above all, the Grimms, discovered and described the German people and their folkways. This movement occurred primarily before the political reaction of 1815. After that date Görres and Brentano retired to a quiet, unproductive life of mystical speculation; and those who remained in active life such as the Grimms and Uhland had unending trouble with academic authorities. Others emigrated. Heine and Börne went to Paris; Alexander von Humboldt travelled through South America, Mexico, Java, and other exotic lands; Chamisso took a trip around the world. Except in the first two cases, this tendency to expatriation cannot be attributed directly to political circumstance; but there does seem to have been a definite trend for the German intellectual to expand his perspective by more travel abroad.

Such is Waiblinger's case, and we have already seen that the reasons for his trip to Italy were numerous. When he went to Italy, he carried with him all that he had learned from Schwab and Uhland; and he was prepared to meet the people and to interpret them to Germany as the romanticists had discovered Germans for Germany. In addition, he was not merely a tool for the romanticists in the execution of their program, but he was also a member of the new generation that fostered a new type of internationalism and discouraged cheap chauvinism, although reserving a healthy respect for the dignity of national traditions. Waiblinger's interest in the Italian people is not to be considered in the light of any school of literature or thought, but strictly as an individual matter, the efforts of one man to find and interpret another culture.

In Italy Waiblinger found a land that, in many respects, had been changeless through the centuries. Whether in Rome or in the country, he was delighted to find a people little different from those of two thousand years ago, and he constantly cited the ancient authors to support this point. His sly comment on Roman women:

Alte Sitt' ist heilig: die Frau gab dem Manne den Schlachthelm

Einst auf das Haupt, und noch jetzt reicht sie den Kopfputz
    ihm dar.[2]

is remarkably similar to the more serious complaint of Juvenal
in his "Vision of Foul Women:"

Tarpeium limen adora
    pronus et auratam Iunoni caede iuvencam,
        si tibi contigerit capitis matrona pudici.[3]

When he travelled in Latium he was constantly reminded of the
simple life portrayed by Livy in the early books of his history
and the parallels that he found in the Italian countryside.   En
route to Naples he described wayside companions who might
have had a rôle in Horace's "Trip to Brindisi".

In addition to the eternal Italy, there was further inspiration
for his lively interest in the people.   One of his favorite literary
exercises was to draw a contrast between Italians and Germans
with didactic intent.   For example:

Italiäner und Deutscher sind nie vereinbare Pole,
    Jener ist ein Kind, dieser dagegen nie.[4]

With a wry smile he commented on the easy morals of Italian
women and at the same time satirized the excessive prudery of
the middle class German:

Zucht und Sittlichkeit wohnt in Deutschland, aber Italien
    Ist der Freude, der Lust, üppiger Sinnlichkeit Land.
O welch ein Unterschied, ein moralischer! Dort sind die H. . . .
    Jungfern und Mädchen, in Rom haben sie gar einen Mann.[5]

Waiblinger learned to appreciate the Italian people as per-
sonalities and to initiate himself into their habits and traditions.
He was impressed by the phrase "dolce far niente" as the most
beautiful sounds in the language.   Once he heard of a baker who
dwelt all his life on the Piazza Rusticucci and never took the
trouble to cross the square and visit St. Peter's.   Waiblinger
commemorated the anecdote with an epigram on "Römische
Faulheit:"

Zwanzig Jahre wohn' ich nun schon auf dem Platze St. Peters,
    Doch in die Kirche hinein kam ich per bacco noch nicht.[6]

The poet enjoyed a little fun over the deadly feud of the
Trasteverini and the Montigiani, although many a foreigner
might have condemned it as a barbarian custom of a degenerate

---

2. *Gedichte aus Italien*, II, 86.
3. *Sat.* VI, 42-44.
4. *Gedichte aus Italien*, II, 89.
5. *Ibid.*
6. *Ibid.*, p. 91.

people. He wrote about the Trasteverini with a well developed sense of humor:

> Wir sind die einzigen Römer, dem Montigianer Verachtung!
> Wir sind noch frei, im Moment stösst man ihm's Messer im Leib.[7]

Roman diversions offered him as much pleasure as any native might have derived from them:

> Corse, Theater und Akademie, Oktober und Giostra,
> Essen und Trinken, man lebt einzig, damit man's geniesst.[8]

At the festival of October he joined the people at the Villa Borghese outside of the city to eat and drink and watch the *saltarello*, the national dance of the Romans:

> Weg mit der Arbeit! Man fährt an den Monte Testaccio, man jubelt,
> Tanzet und spielet und trinkt, bis der Oktober vergeht.[9]

Waiblinger even preferred to go hungry than to miss the festivities:

> Lieber drei Wochen gehungert, und dann mit wallender Feder,
> Tamburin und Gesang nur zum Testaccio hinaus.[10]

Waiblinger's observations on Italian women are more extensive than on any other group or class of Italians. He had several liaisons with Italian women,[11] and during the last two years of his life he lived with a widow whom he called "Cornacchia" (the crow) and who bore two of his children. Frey, who had access to unpublished letters to Eser, has described the ideal relationship of the couple with special emphasis on Waiblinger's appreciation of her typical Italian characteristics:

> Wenn je, so hat Waiblinger dem ganzen Zauber ehelichen und häuslichen Glückes in den ersten Sommermonaten des Jahres 1828 empfunden. Er hatte sich wieder, wie im vorhergehenden Jahre, von den Deutschen zurückgezogen und lebte in verborgener Stille ganz nur seiner Freundin, die er scherzweise Cornacchia, zuweilen auch Carlenza nennt. Als junge Frau, deren Mann seinerzeit mit einer Engländerin durchgebrannt war, hatte sie sich Waiblinger bald mit all der Aufopferung und Anhänglichkeit eines getäuschten Herzens hingegeben, das in der zweiten Leidenschaft die Schmach der ersten auszulöschen versucht. Aus ihr schaute die echte Römerin mit üppigem, kohlrabenschwarzem Haar und feurigen Augen, nur wurde sie leicht etwas zu hitzig, so dass sie zehnmal des Tags sich streiten und wieder versöhnen konnte. Aber dafür war ihr auch jene natürliche Frische der Italienerinnen, grosse Güte des Herzens und überhaupt eine gesunde, kräftige Weiblichkeit eigens. Sie liebte, und die Liebe füllte ihr stolzes Herz so aus, dass sie an eine formelle Heirat weiter gar nicht dachte, sondern unbesorgt nur ihrem Glücke lebte. Trefflich verstand sie

---

7. *Ibid.*, p. 90.
8. *Ibid.*, p. 89.
9. *Ibid.*, p. 90.
10. *Ibid.*
11. Frey, p. 98, refers to Waiblinger's pride in his amatory prowess.

es, den Geliebten an sich zu gewöhnen, ohne ihm lästig zu fallen.
Sie machte ihn geordnet, nahm ihm die Sorgen für kleinliche
Äusserlichkeiten ab, ja, sie hätte ihn am liebsten beständig um sich
behalten . . . Der Brief vom 8. Juli 1828 an Eser beginnt mit einem
wahren Jubelschrei: "Sì! mio cuore! io sono felice! La prima volta
lo posse dire senza paura d'ingannarmi! Perchè questa mia felicità
nonè fondata nel cieco calore d'una sfrenata passione, or in un
sogno piuttosta poetico che essenziale, ma nell' armonia interna,
la quale mi restituisce a me ed a tutto il mondo, volesse l'Iddio,
per sempre!" . . . Nicht ohne Grund schreibt Waiblinger seinem
Eser über dieses ihr tägliches Leben: "Così mio cuore, posse dire,
che benchè mi manchi il genio di Goethe, non mi manchi lo sua
felicità romana!"[12]

Waiblinger saw in Cornacchia his ideal of the Italian woman,
hot-tempered and yet capable of the tenderest emotions. He
took his special pleasure in the Italian atmosphere of life with
Cornacchia; and in this respect he differed from Goethe, who
saw in Faustine the incarnation of southern life, but did not
look upon her as distinctly Italian.

Waiblinger always sought in other women the same things
that appealed to him in Cornacchia. His "Lieder der Nazar-
ena"[13] give the bare descriptive details of an idyllic affair amid
a flood of tender lyricism in which the emotions of an Italian
village maiden are quite obvious. His travel sketches are full
of amusing little affairs (probably not too serious after his
affection for Cornacchia ripened). His stories are full of
Italian women whom he treats in quite realistic fashion.

There are two canons for the beauty of Italian women which
Waiblinger composed to accompany engravings he selected for
his published writings. Both are reproduced in the collected
works. The first engraving, entitled "Die Römerin" is at the
beginning of the fourth volume of the collected works and was
originally an illustration for *Die heilige Woche* (in the *Taschenbuch aus Italian und Griechenland auf das Jahr 1829*); and
Waiblinger has given us an effective appraisal of her charms:

. . . wem ist das römische Profil nicht bekannt? Und dennoch kommen so viele belesene und gebildete Fremde, kommen sogar viele
Künstler nach Rom, und treffen ein ganz anderes Frauengeschlecht,
als sie sich's entweder mit der Willkür ihrer Einbildungskraft
oder nach falschen Darstellungen vor's Auge gebracht. Besonders,
wer die Reise nach Rom über Paris gemacht, wer die Reize eines
koketten Anzugs und französischen Benehmens, wer die schlanke
Taille der Engländerin, wer die weisse Gesichtsfarbe, den senti-
mentalen Ausdruck unserer schönen Landsmänninnen als Richt-
schnur in der Beurtheilung weiblicher Schönheit annimmt, der sucht
vergebens auf der Strasse, im Theater, im Festino, in der Akademie,

---

12. *Ibid.*, p. 208-209.
13. *Gedichte aus Italien*, I, 53-67.

in den Feuerwerken des Mausoleums eine Römerin, welche seinen Erwartungen genügen könnte. Sie ist ihm zu derb, zu kräftig, selbst zu unzart, ja unweiblich, ihr Wuchs zu ungefällig, zu grandios, ihr Angesicht zeigt weder Milch und Blut, noch die Empfindung einer Deutschen, ihr Anzug weder den Geschmack, den er im Palais royal bewundert, noch den Reichthum, welcher die Brittin auszeichnet, ja wir haben schon von Deutschen und Franzosen, besonders aber von Engländern sagen hören, dass die Römerinnen geradezu das plumpste Weibergeschlecht auf Erden seyen.[14]

Waiblinger had little sympathy with hypercritical travellers who failed to appreciate the better points of Italian women and contrasted them with their own countrywomen in respect to artificial decorations and material wealth. Waiblinger saw in the Roman woman a natural simplicity that did not occur in a sophisticated salon of Paris, and yet he understood that this type of beauty might not have a universal appeal. He closed his little sketch with a remark on the shapely figures of Italian women, not forbidden by any northern prudery to clothe themselves lightly.

In many of Waiblinger's works in which there is art criticism, he frequently revealed the influence of the neo-classicism of Canova and his school. Such is the case with the introductory statement on another engraving of an Italian woman, "Die Genzaneserin," which appears at the beginning of the eighth volume of his collected works.[15] His characterization of her beauty was in line with the efforts of contemporary artists to revive the spirit of antiquity:

. . . und so sind wir im Stande, dir, lieber Leser, ein ziemlich getreues Abbild eines Kopfes zu übergeben, dessen grandioser Geist, dessen ideale Formen die schönen Frauen des Albanergebirges im Allgemeinen auf's würdigste charakterisiren kann. Suchst du Formen, wie sie die alten Künstler aus der reichen südlichen Natur auslasen, um daraus jene vollkommenen Ideale zu erschaffen, welche wir noch in den unsterblichen Denkmälern der Vorzeit bewundern und nachahmen, ohne ihnen nur gleichkommen, geschweige sie übertreffen zu können; liegt es dir daran, den Charakterkopf einer Frau kennen zu lernen, wie wir sie in üppiger, frischer Gesundheit, in seltener Kraft und Stärke in den Gegenden von Albano, Genzano, Frascati, oder auch in den Gebirgen der Sabiner, in jenen himmelhohen Felsennestern in den Umgebungen von Subiaco und Olevano finden. . .[16]

---

14. *Werke*, IV, i.

15. This illustration was originally printed in the "Supplementblatt" of the *Stuttgarter Abendzeitung*, nos. 52-58, 1-6 March 1827. The original was an oil painting by the German artist Grahl, who prepared it for an exposition of the works of German artists in Rome in honor of King Ludwig of Bavaria in 1827. Waiblinger states that much life and color was lost in the engraving.

16. *Werke*, VIII, i.

Despite his desire to find a reincarnation of the classic type, the poet realized that after all such women might actually be found in modern Italy. He felt that they displayed their beauty to best advantage against native scenery rather than in lifeless marble.

Waiblinger entertained liberal ideas about the easy morals of Italian women, but he was not able to adapt himself to every situation. On one occasion in Frascati he was strongly attracted by a young woman who repulsed him with the stock, "Dopo che io sono sposata, ma non primo."[17] Still he praised the Italian woman who insisted on protecting her honor.[18] While Waib-linger, like Catullus, could sing high admiration for the virtuous woman, he was equally capable of writing bitterly satirical verses on the woman of few moral scruples:

> Immer spricht man vom Joch des Ehstands, wann denn vertauscht man
> Endlich das Bild und setzt Hörner des Ehstands dafür?[19]

or:

> Eingezogen und sittsam verfliesst die Zeit mir als Jungfrau,
> Ist die Hochzeit vorbei, fängt das Commercium erst an.[20]

Waiblinger, whose youth was filled with excesses, had matured and learned to know the Italian people so well that he is able to give an objective account of the vices as well as the virtues of Italian women.

Waiblinger found Italian men, in general, a merry lot, think-ing more about *panem et circenses* than about the weightier problems of life, but he did not view them as the effeminate characters we know in cheap fiction. His Italian is a colorful individual, and the poet often forced this point with a contrast between the German and the Italian, for example, in a humorous sally on Roman gluttony and German drunkenness:

> Was ein Römer isst, und ein Deutscher trinket, das dünkt mir,
> Wär' am Ende sogar Gullivers Riesen genug.[21]

He described these gentlemen as the lords of heaven and earth in their contentment with life:

> Wir sind die Herrn, wir haben den Schlüssel zu Himmel und Erde,
> Keine Schatulle, der er, wenn sie nur voll ist, nicht passt.[22]

---

17. *Ibid.,* p. 2.
18. *E.g., Gedichte aus Italien,* I, 60.
19. *Gedichte aus Italien,* II, 91.
20. *Ibid.,* p. 90.
21. *Ibid.,* II, 85.
22. *Ibid.*

A long parade of Italian men pass in review in Waiblinger's works. There are peasants, artists, Roman street rabble, gentlemen of leisure, entertainers, and tradesmen. Perhaps the most striking are his peasants, who appear all through the travel sketches. He found in them many of the same general characteristics that are attributed to the northern European peasant: sly trickery, good-natured fun making, suspicious attitudes toward strangers, and a confirmed belief in the goodness of their own life. On the other hand, they are hardly models of thrift, or, to put the idea more broadly, of the old Roman *frugalitas*. Their extravagance is typified in the *improvisatore* Michel Angelo, who went out every night after he had earned a little money and spent it on strong drink to loosen his tongue and thereby enhance his poetic gifts.[23] Typical of the limited outlook of the Italian peasant are the verses that Waiblinger copied from a peasant's door:

> Jo devo morire, e non so dove,
> Jo devo morire, e non so quando.
> Jo devo morire, e non so come.[24]

Naturally there follows the unexpressed although quite logical thought of *carpe diem* in the commentary on these fatalistic lines, a peasant trait which Waiblinger also portrayed in his vivid scenes from the nightly festivities in the local *osteria*.

Along with the peasant Waiblinger always found the village priest to be a man who shared the basic characteristics of his parishioners. Typical is the abbot of Palestrina:

> Der Abbate von Palestrina, der eine besondere Passion für mich gewonnen, wollte mich heute mit einem Besuch beehren: ich sass aber auf meinem Felsen aussen im Ospidale und vergegenwärtigte mir noch einmal meinen ganzen Aufenthalt in diesen Hernikerbergen, mit allen Freuden und Leiden, mit Furcht und Hoffnung, und allen seinen guten oder schlimmen Folgen. Den Abend aber erwischte er mich im Caffe. Ich schaute einer lustigen Scene hier zu. Einige Kapuziner von St. Francesco in Civitella kamen, und zogen dem Caffeewirth einen Zahn heraus. Der Abbate war erfreut, und bat mich, mit ihm einen kleinen Spaziergang zu machen. Er schien mir ein wenig Libertin zu seyn. Endlich aber drang er auf's heftigste in mich, meine Abreise auf Übermorgen zu verschieben, und den kommenden Tag ihm zu widmen. Ich entschuldigte mich mit der Unmöglichkeit, allein er liess keine Gründe gelten. Als wir in der Dämmerung nach Hause kamen, rief uns Domenico, der Vater, einen lustigen Gruss zu, und verrieth Weinhitze. Ich bat den Abbate, mit mir zu kommen, und Angelo besorgte eine Bocchia Wein; auf der Loggia wurde er getrunken. Der Abbate erwies mir alle möglichen Höflichkeiten und drang immer

23. *Werke*, VIII, 224 *et seq.*
24. *Ibid.*, p. 212.

gewaltsamer in mich, zu bleiben. Zuletzt verrieth er sich und ich merkte, dass der Grund seiner eminenten Passion für mich, Liebe zur Poesie war, die auch er, wie er sagte, zuweilen nur bei Gelegenheit treibe.[25]

Waiblinger was particularly fond of participating in rural fiestas, for here he found the true spirit of *dolce far niente*. During the last days of his summer visit to Olevano in 1828 he was present at such a festival and described it with sympathy and enthusiasm.[26]

Waiblinger's interest in the men of the cities was related to his attitude toward the peasant. He observed the evil traits of the Italian city dweller such as meanness and untrustworthiness, but he found one redeeming feature, his zest for life so typical of his nationality. Night life in Rome appealed strongly to Waiblinger, particularly when he was able to participate personally. He took the greatest pleasure in following a certain sausage dealer who enjoyed a local reputation as an *improvisatore*, often until three or four in the morning.[27] Again, he liked to indulge in the carefree Bohemian atmosphere of Rome, a city of freedom and romantic adventures at that time without the modern bustle. At the Café Greco he felt perfectly at home among the German and Italian artists who frequented the place:

Dutzende sitzen beisammen in uralt' römischer Höhle,
    Kaum durch ein düsteres Loch stiehlt hier der Tag sich herein,
Unser Mahl ist frugal, doch trinken wir gern und im Dampfe
    Derben Tabakes vergisst leicht man den heimlichen Feind.[28]

Still he took special delight in his association with Italian men by mixing with the lowest groups. We have an intimate picture of the so-called *minenti*[29] on a hot summer day gathered in the Temple of Peace to pass the time:

Um Vergebung, der Tag ist zu heiss, und ein Haufen Minenti
    Findet's im Heiligthum selber zum Mora bequem.[30]

Little details like this appear constantly in the poet's works, and it is clear that he not only appreciated the life of the average

---

25. *Ibid.*, p. 241-142.
26. *Ibid.*, p. 279-280.
27. *Gedichte aus Italien*, II, 169.
28. *Ibid.*, p. 44.
29. The *minenti* were from the lowest social groups and were distinguished by a special costume, *viz.*, a round hat, a Manchester jacket hung carelessly over one shoulder, and a sash around the middle. They were frequently contrasted with the *baine*, who dressed in French style. See *Gedichte aus Italien*, II, 169.
30. *Ibid.*, p. 80. *Mora* is a kind of finger play of the Italians with which they amuse themselves hours at a time.

Italian but that he had also participated in the daily round of activity.

Waiblinger was no less interested in the customs and traditions of the Italian people. To be sure, he executed for them no such monumental works as the Grimm brothers did in the field of German folklore and antiquities, but he did display broad interest in the customs of the people. He made no great collection of folksongs, but he frequently noted catchy verses and good improvisations with such care that any careful investigation of the Italian folksong should take his work into account. Nor did he collect proverbs, tales, and local traditions in any scientific manner, but this material is found everywhere in his work.

We have already noted Waiblinger's interest in such folk artists as the *improvisatori*. He was no less interested in the drunken Michel Angelo improvising atop a rocky crag in the Alban hills than he was in the more sophisticated performances of Rosa Taddei and the Cavaliere Sgricci. If he lacked the money to travel or the necessary prestige for admission to an academy, he would stand on the street corner to watch for any fortuitous item of interest.[31] Even here he never failed to find some folk artist. It might be the lowly sausage dealer whose improvisations were locally famous, or it might be a puppet show, where the *improvisatori* combined their poetic gifts with dramatic talent.[32] The *burratini* or marionettes were set up in Waiblinger's day in vacant lots and unfrequented alleys throughout Rome. There were usually six or seven characters supporting Cassandro and Pulcinella in all manner of slapstick, and they always had large audiences.

Waiblinger paid due attention to Italian legends. We have noted his tendency to give the ancient Roman legends a modern background to show their full significance for modern Italy. The legends of mediaeval and Renaissance Italy do not figure as prominently in his work as do the legends of antiquity. Occasionally Waiblinger may introduce a miracle of St. Francis,[33] or he will repeat the pretty story that Tasso died under a great oak on the Gianicolo where he had climbed for

---

31. "Mein Vergnügen ist . . . Hab' ich kein Geld mehr, so pflanz' ich an die Ecke mich auf." *Ibid.*, p. 89.
32. *Ibid.*
33. *Werke*, VIII, 9.

a final panorama of his country.[34] Again we have the story that
the Romans insist that the beauty of Andrea del Sarto's
madonnas was simply an escape complex acquired from life
with a nagging wife; or we read a prank of Bartoldo, the Italian
Nesreddin Hoca.[35]

The aspect of Italian life that appealed to Waiblinger above
all else was the continual atmosphere of fiesta. Goethe appreciated the carnivals, but even in his indulgences he revealed a
restraint that Waiblinger never knew. Goethe saw in the
Roman carnival the brilliance of a southern land as contrasted
with the gloom of melancholy Germany, whereas Waiblinger
expanded this idea to a conception of the carnival as an absolute
virtue of the Roman people.

The best evidence for Waiblinger's love of Italian festivities
is his "Lieder des Römischen Carnevals," which he composed
in 1828. Here he described all the color and the merry-making
of the carnival season in a highly exuberant tone. At the very
beginning of the collection he offered his reasons for choosing
the carnival as a poetic theme:

> Und warum nicht, heitere Muse,
> Lied und Lob dem Carnevale?
> Bienen könntest du besingen,
> Könntest schöne Frauen ehren,
> Selbst den Duft der Blumen preisen—
> Und warum nicht all die Schwärme
> Lust'ger, honigsüsser Feen,
> Rom in Kränzen und in Blumen?[36]

He provided all the necessary orientation for a full appreciation
of the carnival:

> Nur ein flüchtiger Bewohner
> Dieser Welt, zum Scherz geboren,
> Zum Moment, will er sein Dasein,
> Gleich dem Schmetterling geniessen,
> Und dem dumpfen Haus der Puppe
> In vollendeter Entfaltung
> Nun entnommen, flattert er
> Buhlend unter seinen Blumen.[37]

This festival was unlike the procession of distinguished
prelates in a church celebration or the exclusive atmosphere of a
brilliant society ball, for here democracy reigned supreme.
Aristocrats rubbed shoulders with plebeians, and all social classes
were completely obsessed by the carnival spirit:

---

34. *Gedichte aus Italien*, I, 93.
35. *Werke*, IX, 17.
36. *Gedichte aus Italien*, I, 13.
37. *Ibid.*, p. 15.

Armuth gibt's nicht mehr und Reichthum.
Eine Maske deckt sie beide,
Und geduldig nimmst du jeden,
Wie er scheint; Gesicht und Hülle,
Wort und die Geberde täuschen.
Die Geschlechter selbst, das Alter
Lächelt dich in Locken an,
Und die Jugend geht an Krücken.[38]

The poet was attracted by the different costumes and the numerous amusing incidents at carnival time. He saw attractive young women who assumed unusual liberties sanctioned by the season, but allowed no extraordinary freedom to men:

Holde, junge Gärtnerinnen
Reichen Veilchen aus den Körben,
Und die breite Arlecchina
Fliegt mit Schellenklang vorüber!
Wie das weisse Hemdchen jene,
Wie die Busenschärpe kleidet!
Bleibe Fern! Nimm dich in Acht,
Ihre Scheeren sind gefährlich![39]

Waiblinger described the carnival with well chosen metaphors such as the one involving the butterfly, and his jocular, half-serious expressions were consistent with the spirit of the carnival. He wrote with such ease that he left the impression of a genuine experience in the record of his participation in the crowning event of Roman life.

Another festival of which Waiblinger was unusually fond was the floral celebration in Genzano, an annual affair at the summer solstice, and he has provided a compact description of the pageantry in a note to one of his poems:

Am 21sten Juni lockt das Blumenfest in Genzano die Bewohner der ganzen Umgebung, ja sogar von Terracina und von den Seestädten, besonders auch die Fremden in Rom an diesem Wohnsitz des ewigen Frühlings zusammen. Dieses Fest ist einer begeisterten Dichterschilderung an anderm Ort wert. Für uns Nordländer scheint es eine Fabel, ein Märchen zu sein. Die Strassen sind von den schönsten Blumen übersäet, mit welchen alle möglichen Zeichnungen, Tempel, Gärten, Altäre, Wappen, Arabesken und Ornamente auf der Fläche ausgeführt sind. Auf ihnen wandeln die Schönheiten Albano's und dieses ganzen glücklichen Landstriches, Profile, deren Hoheit und Charakter an Niobe erinnern, die überaus reiche und reizende Tracht dieser antiken Frauen, die vielen andern Kostüme vom Meer her, welche orientalischen Geschmack haben, die Gesundheit, Fülle, Kraft und Frische in diesem weiblichen Heldengeschlecht, der Jubel den ganzen Tag über, die angefüllten Strassen, die tumultuarischen Osterien, die Bekannten die man findet, der köstliche Wein, nahezu der beste im ganzen Kirchenstaat, und vorzüglich die elysäische Natur, die immergrünen Eichenhaine, die Pappelufer des Sees von Nemi, die herr-

38. *Ibid.*, p. 17.
39. *Ibid.*, p. 20.

liche Meeraussicht—das alles kommt zusammen, um einen solchen
Tag unvergesslich zu machen.[40]

Das Blumenfest is a weak story in most respects, but a contemporary critic praised Waiblinger's successful use of local
color against a plausible sixteenth century background with the
statement that ". . . sie zu den italienischen Novellen der deutschen Erzähler sich verhalte wie wirkliche Blumen zu italienischen."[41] The plot of the story is quite fantastic, and the one
redeeming feature is Waiblinger's intimate and realistic picture
of the carnival.

At the beginning of the fifth volume of the collected works
there is a copper engraving illustrating the flower festival in
Genzano. Like the others, it first appeared with the author's
explanation in the *Taschenbuch auf das Jahr 1829*. The picture
is entitled "Ländliches Fest im Kirchenstaat", and it shows a
large number of country people gathered in a courtyard where
there is about to be a dramatic representation of some religious
interest. The inevitable Arlequino is outside dressed in a
clown's costume and going through his repertory to attract a
crowd while the spieler is pointing to some important episode
in the drama shown on a large picture hung up against the side
of a building. The original, a painting by Mlle. Lescot, appears
to have been done with all the graphic realism of the Hogarth
tradition; and it must have left a strong impression on Waiblinger in his constant search for incidents from the life of the
people.

Another significant engraving heads the seventh volume of
the collected works. It is entitled "Der Vorleser in Neapel,"
and, appropriately enough, it is at the beginning of the volume
containing Waiblinger's poetry. A motley group has gathered
around an old sailor who has taken his stand on an open wharf
to declaim poetry for whatever pittance his audience may be
willing to contribute. We are told that the old fellow is reading
or reciting from Ariosto, and a special point is made of the
Italian's natural appreciation of poetry.[42] This enthusiasm
for a popular literature was completely in harmony with the
ideas that had been presented in northern Europe by the pre-

---

40. *Ibid.*, p. 108. The second sentence refers to *Das Blumenfest,* in
Werke, III, 79-219.
41. *Apud* Ruland, p. 51.
42. *Werke*, VII, i-ii.

ceding generation, but in addition we have here the conception of natural poetic genius innate in the Italian people. Even if the old sailor were an exception to the ordinary run of humanity, his remarkable audience would seem to prove for Waiblinger that even those Italians who did not possess the gift of declamation were capable of appreciating the best in poetry:

> Höchst anmuthig dünkt uns die Gruppe der drei Lazzaronen zu seyn, welche wir oben als die regelmässigsten Skolaren bezeichnet. Jener mit dem Strohhut raucht sein Pfeifchen in voller Behaglichkeit, für einen halben Gran so köstliche Dinge von Helden und Schlachten, Königen und Mohren, Zauberern und Kastellen zu hören; die beiden andern gaffen den Vorleser mit offenem Mund an, nicht ohne Respekt vor dem trefflichen Manne, der so vollkommen zu lesen versteht.[43]

Waiblinger has accentuated this picture of everyday Neapolitan life by bringing out not only the carefree nature of an audience none too hospitable to work but also the natural feeling for poetry which he assumed to be inherent in every Italian.

Other scenes reflecting the Italian bent for indulgence in play rather than in serious work are numerous in Waiblinger's works. The scenes that have already been mentioned are representative of what may be found in the tales, poems, and travel sketches. Six of the eight engravings chosen by Waiblinger to accompany his *Italienisches Taschenbuch für 1829* represent scenes from Italian life or interesting individuals whom he encountered in Italy, and three of them depict the atmosphere of the carnival.[44]

Somewhat less important than the material on the Italian people contained in Waiblinger's lyrical and journalistic works are the Italian characters in the tales. None of Waiblinger's fiction is of great significance in the history of the German *Novelle*, but in certain details some pieces show how Waiblinger was gradually approaching literary maturity. He was a lyric poet at his best; and, like many other Swabian poets, his dramas and tales suffer in comparison. Accordingly we must not expect the realism and careful detail in scenes from Italian life that we have found elsewhere. Many isolated points such as Waiblinger's use of the *improvisatori* and the carnival atmosphere in his tales

43. *Ibid.*, p. iii-iv.
44. An engraving of a scene from *Das Märchen von der blauen Grotte* is in vol. III, and a picture of Tenerani's statue of Cupid and Venus is in vol. VI. Vol. IV contains "Die Römerin," and vol. VIII contains "Die Genzaneserin." Vol. II has an engraving illustrating the contemptuous attitude of Englishmen toward Italians. The three illustrating Italians at play are "Ländliches Fest im Kirchenstaat" (vol. V), "Der Vorleser in Neapel" (vol. VII), and "Die Piferari" (vol. IX).

have been discussed in other connections, and here we will examine only those typically Italian traits and situations which the poet used in the delineation of his characters. Moreover, this material is interesting in comparison with two of Waiblinger's earliest works, *Phaethon* and *Liebe und Hass*, both of which are set in the south, one in Greece and the other in Italy. The latter is a motley combination of characters and episodes that Waiblinger found in such works as *Romeo and Juliet*, *Emilia Galotti*, and the *Räuberromane* dealing with life in wildest Italy. The later tales, however lacking in psychological motivation, are afflicted with no such unrealistic ideas about Italy.

Die heilige Woche presents a Roman painter and his family as typical Italians, and, significantly enough, it bears the sub-title, "Charactergemälde aus Rom." The characters, especially the women, are drawn clearly and objectively in contrast with several Germans who are in the story. The wife of the painter is a hot-blooded, impetuous woman who is infatuated with Eduard and forgets all marital responsibilities in her efforts to win his love. One lively scene depicts her in the midst of the *tarantella* calculated to excite Eduard to return her advances. A pretty servant girl and the children reflect the older woman's fiery Italian personality in minor details.

Das Blumenfest is a historical tale, and the characters are fictitious, but still they display certain traditional Italian traits. Vittoria, the peasant sweetheart of Prince Giulio, is perhaps the outstanding character. She is proud and emotional, yet her magnanimous behavior toward her lover and her boldness in affairs of the heart set her off as a typical Italian woman similar to the wife of the painter in *Die heilige Woche*. Her mother is also an Italian type. She shows considerable apprehension for the good name of her daughter, and her conduct on the occasion of the visit of Prince Giulio's father is marked by feelings of fear and respect. Finally we have the impoverished shepherd· Cecco who has gambled and drunk away his patrimony until he is reduced to a bottle of bad wine and a couple of volumes of his favorite poet. Yet he is happy with these poor belongings, for even when they are gone he can still amuse himself with his improvisations. It is interesting to note in this tale that Waiblinger was at his best in his portrayal of folk characters rather than aristocrats.

Of the three serious stories with an Italian background,

Francesco Spina is probably the weakest, since it was composed quickly as hack work. None of the main characters are from the humbler classes. An aristocratic lady, a Spaniard, a German, and an Italian painter are the chief characters, and even the last is weak. Still, we have an earthy figure of a bandit chieftain and a sly rustic who earns a double fee for guiding Emil and Francesco to the Villa of Horace. Oda, the Spaniard, is a somewhat inappropriate individual to be endowed with the gift of improvisation, while the bandit fits the same role quite naturally.

The humorous stories, *Das Abenteuer von der Sohle* and *Die Britten in Rom,* introduce Italians as subordinate figures. In the former the artist Scaramuzza is a typical figure from the bohemian life in Rome that Waiblinger knew so well. *Die Britten in Rom* is quite interesting as a satire on the Englishman on the *grand tour.* The Englishmen, among whom Waiblinger himself figures as Ironius, take unfair advantage of the poverty-stricken Romans and show no respect for human values.

Waiblinger's tales are not as effective in illustrating Italian character as his other writings are, but we find much that is valuable in them, especially such unusual figures as *improvisatori,* artists, and bandits. Frequently he shows lack of discipline in letting his imagination run riot in these characterizations; and the essential lack of merit in his tales is responsible for many of his shoddy characters. His characters drawn from the aristocracy are the poorest of all, and, unfortunately, most of the chief figures in his tales come from this source. Most of his interesting Italian characters are subordinate.

On the whole, however, Waiblinger was original, constructive, enthusiastic, and well acquainted with the people among whom he spent his last years and who figure so largely in his works. In his fairness to the Italian people he was able to pick out both vices and virtues of Italian character, and he defended Italians as a loyal friend against the scorn of other foreigners. In discussing their vices he rarely spoke with too sharp a tongue, and he disguised his criticism with a veil of good humor.

Waiblinger's consistent effort to interpret Italy to his German readers and his natural love of the Italian people are perhaps his most important characteristics as an author. He liked to contrast German dullness with Italian vivacity, German philistinism with Italian bohemianism, German pedantry with Italian originality. He found in Italy his lost horizon of escape from

all that he disliked in Germany just as Goethe and Zacharias
Werner had before him; and like Goethe, but unlike Werner, he
never forgot his native land and his task of bringing to her whatever good Italy could offer. He would not attempt to graft any
unnatural custom or tradition on the German stem, for he had
learned the great lesson of his age, recognition of the legitimacy
of all national cultures. He showed that Italy had a folklore
comparable to anything excavated from German tradition by the
romantic folklorists. He referred constantly to the legends of
antiquity, he gave encyclopaedic information on Italian women,
and he described Italian festivals with tireless enthusiasm. Everywhere he sought traces of folk art and folk artists.

Waiblinger found his *Schlaraffenland* in Italy. His case has
few parallels as a man who found a second home in Italy and
lived intimately with the people as one of them. He was not only
in a better position to interpret the Italian people for Germany,
but he also found a haven and sympathetic friends for his own
südliche Natur. Hölderlin never got beyond Provence in the
search for his idealized Greece, Byron was disappointed in what
he actually found, and Lenau's gypsy blood drove him to seek the
noble savage in America, where he too was disillusioned. Waiblinger expressed most poignantly his spiritual satisfaction and
his happiness among the Italian people in the "Oden an seinen
Eser."[45] Here we feel that the happiness he found with his Cornacchia could not have been attained in life with the prudish
Philippine Heim or with the unstable Julie Michaelis. Italy did
not prove a false illusion to him, nor was he untrue to her once
he had established congenial relationships with her people.

---

45. *Gedichte aus Italien*, II, 108-113.

CHAPTER VI

WAIBLINGER AND ANTIQUITY

Although Waiblinger may have explored some new facets of Italian life and culture unknown in northern Europe, no traveller in Italy since the Renaissance failed to give due attention to the remains of classical times. Above all, it was Roman antiquity that attracted men of the sixteenth and seventeenth centuries, for the old lands of Magna Graecia were not properly described by moderns until the age of Winckelmann. Although Waiblinger frequently grouped Greek and Roman antiquity together as a part of the general dichotomy of north and south so popular in his day, his interests in Greece and in Rome spring from different sources and, accordingly, will be handled differently here.

Von Klenze gives a typical reaction to Italy in his summary of Montaigne's visit: "Only ancient Rome inspires him to a burst of enthusiasm worthy of so great a stylist."[1] Even narrower was Joseph Addison's approach to Italy and Roman antiquity, for the worthy author of *Coins and Medals* found inspiration only in places mentioned by the Latin poets, ignoring almost completely the prose authors. Horace Walpole and Lalande, the French traveller, found every step of the way between Rome and Naples sacred primarily because of associations with Horace, Virgil, and Silius Italicus.

In the late eighteenth and early nineteenth centuries the conception of Italy was broadened considerably, but there still remained the eternal attraction of ancient Rome. Chateaubriand could dream of how "Rome sommeille au milieu de ses ruines,"[2] for the romanticists were still spellbound by Rome. Waiblinger fell heir not only to the romantic tradition, but also to the ideas of travellers of nearly three centuries about Rome.

Waiblinger was well prepared to understand the ancient world, for he had acquired unusual proficiency in Latin. He is able to quote extensively from Horace. The well known "Possis nihil urbe Roma visere maius" (*Carm. saec.*, lines 11-12) serves as the motto for "Oden und Elegien aus Rom." At Lake Nemi Waiblinger remembered how the Romans, despairing of victory

1. Von Klenze, p. 2.
2. *Ibid.*, p. 89.

over the Veii, sent to Delphi, where the oracle told the emissaries
to drain off part of the lake by a subterranean tunnel.[3] Waiblinger must have known Roman topography well, for in the letter to
Mörike dated only a few weeks after his arrival in Rome he
showed a comprehensive knowledge of the ruins and their loca-
tions.

Even though Waiblinger went to Italy with a classical background comparable to that of any of his predecessors, he did not
follow beaten paths in his ideas on antiquity. Indeed, the preceding generation had received from Goethe an original and stimula-
ting treatment of Italian antiquities as symbols of a glorious
classicism rather than as museum pieces; and with Waiblinger
we may expect similar originality, although as widely variant
from Goethe's work as Goethe himself was from the travellers
of the Renaissance. Quite early Waiblinger had realized that the
poet might select the most banal themes and the oldest material
for new and original interpretation.[4]

One of the most striking aspects of Waiblinger's treatment
of classicial antiquity is his ability to revive scenes from ancient
Rome against a modern Italian background. We have noted the
little couplet on "Classisches in Tibur"[5] where he found his pleasure in both "Vorwelt und Mitwelt." He saw — or imagined that
he saw — classic profiles in modern Italians, the same landscape
that inspired Horace and Virgil, the same places and temples
that the ancient poets knew, all a part of eternal Italy:

> Da sich die Zukunft eint mit Vergangenheit,
> Beid' aber unvergängliche Gegenwart;
> Ohn' Anfang beid' und ohne Ende,
> Beide die göttliche Ewigkeit sind.[6]

Waiblinger's idea about the reflection of ancient Rome in
modern Italy appears in his treatment of Italian women. In one
of the "Lieder des Römischen Carnevals" there is a description
of a young woman who might have been a worthy consort of
great Zeus:

> Blumen lächeln aus der Haare
> Rabendunkel, und des Schleiers
> Weisse Masse senkt sich üppig
> Auf ein Schulternpaar, wie Marmor,
> Und aus hochgeschwelltem Tuche
> Tritt ein Nacken, dessen Reize

---

3. *Werke*, VIII, 32.
4. *Werke*, IV, 232.
5. *Gedichte aus Italien*, I, 41.
6. *Gedichte aus Italien*, II, 109.

Nur des grossen Donn'rers Arm
Zu umschlingen würdig scheinet.[7]

When the gaily clad mob began to indulge in all the joys of the carnival, the poet envisioned the women as modern maenads:

Weisse freudentrunkne Mädchen,
Arlecchine und Doctoren,
Gärtnerinnen und Bajacci,
Und der plumpe Pulcinella,
Leichte Schäfer, farb'ge Türken,
Schwarzvermummte, schlanke Feen,
Alles in Mänadenwuth,
Saturnalischem Vergnügen.[8]

The southern beauty of Italian women so strongly reminiscent of antiquity appealed to Waiblinger. The longer he looked at Roman women, the more he believed "eine Lucretia, eine Clölia, eine Cornelia, eine Porzia aus ihnen heraus zu finden,"[9] and in Genzano he saw figures "wie sie die alten Künstler aus der reichen südlichen Natur auslasen."[10]

The whole natural environment recalled antiquity for him. Even one of his early poems such as "Das Pantheon" expressing melancholy and nostalgia shows how an ancient monument could stir him emotionally to the extent of referring to the structure as the "Opferschaale meiner Thränen".[11]

Later, when Waiblinger enjoyed a more stable life in Italy and some degree of financial security, he gave up this early Byronism, and there is nothing but pure joy in his references to antiquity. In Sicily he passed by the Villa of Timoleon and sketched an idyllic scene in which he imagined that he was suddenly transported to the ancient world:

Wär's eine Nymphe, die in der Einsamkeit
Dem Wandrer sich verräth? Im Gebüsch vielleicht
Verborgen lauscht das holde Wesen
Und dem Erschöpften ertönt die Stimme:

Komm, labe, Wandrer, dich und Epipoli
Gestärkt besteigst du![12]

Ancient Rome stamped Italy with a national tradition that cannot be effaced by time. The villages of the Alban hills were not mere hamlets for Waiblinger, but "dreitausendjährige Städte"[13]; and the grotto of Diana on Lago Albano more than simply

7. *Gedichte aus Italien*, I, 19.
8. *Ibid.*, p. 30.
9. *Werke*, IV, ii.
10. *Werke*, VIII ,i.
11. *Gedichte aus Italien*, I, 91-92.
12. *Gedichte aus Italien*, II, 141.
13. *Ibid.*, p. 29.

one of nature's beauty spots, it was "heiliger Boden der Fabelwelt."[14] Whether Waiblinger was visiting some ancient monument or even enjoying the unadorned aspects of the countryside, his images from the ancient world are an important element in his poetry and prose.

When Waiblinger visited the villa of Horace in the spring of 1823, he composed a delightful account of the ancient Sabine farm as a traditional aspect of the Italian landscape. After an amusing experience with a rascally guide he was relieved to rest beside the Bandusian Fountain and repeat the famous ode (*Carm.* III, 13). As he made his arduous way to the villa he remembered the words of Horace in *Epod.* I, 7:

Mihi jam non regia Roma
Sed vacuum Tibur placet!

At any time we may find some reminiscence of antiquity, regardless of present surroundings. Waiblinger showed both the enthusiasm of a Renaissance traveller discovering some vestigial remnant of ancient Rome and the dreamy speculation of his romantic contemporaries. He enjoyed his classical background because it helped him to understand the same eternal Italy that Horace knew. Waiblinger believed that he could appreciate Italy as well as any poet of antiquity.

Most characteristic of this attitude is an account of his visit to Pompeii in 1829. Waiblinger felt at home in the ancient city, and he showed not only the scientific interest of the archaeologist but also the sensitivity of the romanticist for the ancient ruins. The first of the *Briefe über Pompeji* [15] describes the natural setting of the old city with an unusually realistic account of Vesuvius, all calculated to acclimate the reader to the world of the first century of our era. When he arrived in the ancient city, he was overjoyed by scenes of two thousand years ago that revealed all the intimacies of daily life from that period. He felt that he had found the true key to the beauties of antiquity, that here was a summary of all the scattered information about ancient life that he had picked up from his reading of the classics. He showed a background of sound scholarship to temper this enthusiasm, for he carefully inspected inscriptions for whatever explanatory material they offered for the surroundings. When he described a dwelling house, he gave exact details such as we might expect

14. *Ibid.*, p. 19.
15. *Werke*, IX, 246-277.

from a modern investigator. He felt that meticulous examination of the ancient ruins would open the way for a broader understanding of ancient civilization. In the fifth letter, for example, there is a description of a Pompeiian house that brings out essential principles of domestic architecture of the ancients.[10]

Waiblinger probably appreciated his trip to Pompeii as fully as any other single event during his four years in Italy. Ancient culture came to life for him with a vividness that rivals the verses of Martial and Horace, and the German poet acquired a new sense for "der unerschöpfliche Kunstsinn der Alten" that served him well in his study of ancient art. This experience completely reformed his conception of antiquity and gave him a far more substantial classical background than that which appears in the rather unsatisfactory *Phaethon*. After his visit to Pompeii he gave more attention to detail, to fine technical points that form the basis of true understanding.

While Pompeii was more significant to Waiblinger than any other Roman ruin, there were other monuments of ancient Italy that were of importance for him. Usually he created some image illustrating the meaning and importance of the particular ruin. At the sarcophagus of the Scipios we catch a glimpse of the life that surrounded this ancient family which contributed so much to the building of Rome's empire:

> Jubelnder Heere Zug,
> Festtrunkene Völker folgten dem Rossgespann,
> Der Aar vom Donnrer in den Himmeln
> Ueber den Häuptern der Herrn der Erde
>
> Ragt' er, ein Kampfgespiele von stolzer Art,
> Der über Asia, über Brittania,
> Der Korsen Eiland und Lukania,
> Afrika's Reiche den Fittig wölbte.[17]

He rarely composed a strictly descriptive poem, although he did several capable pieces of this sort, notably an epigram on a temple in Cori:

> Bist du des Helden Tempel, der hier dem blumigen Felsen,
> Einem Elysium hier, Myrthen und Rosen entragt,
> Wahrlich dann bauten die Grazien dich, zum lieblichsten Denkmal,
> Dass dir die Göttin den Trank ewiger Jugend gereicht.[18]

More often he had a motive for such descriptions, perhaps to conjure up a forgotten scene or for a satirical purpose. His admiration for the ancient Romans and his dislike for the Trasteverini

---

16. *Ibid.*, p. 261-262.
17. *Gedichte aus Italien*, II, 16-17.
18. *Gedichte aus Italien*, I, 39.

is brought out in an epigram on the stone bridge of M. Fulvius
the Censor:

> Eine zerbrochene Brücke, was ist's kein Wunder am Ende!
> Alles vergeht, und der Welt wird's nicht viel besser geschehn.
> Dererlei merkt man sich nicht, auch wenn die Brücke sich
>   weigert,
> Mit dem gefallnen Geschlecht über die Tiber zu gehn.[19]

As we have seen, much of Waiblinger's early work reflected
a Byronic *Weltschmerz,* for example, his description of the crum-
bling glory of the Campo Vaccino and the Pantheon standing as
a solitary symbol of ancient Rome at her height. As he matured
he was less concerned about the sad state of the ancient Roman
monuments in modern times. In a few short verses on the temple
of Jupiter Stator he tells of triumphant Rome ruling the world
with Augustus at the helm:

> Dir erbaute das siegende Rom, o Jupiter Stator,
> Dankbar ein Säulenhaus, weil du es siegen gelehrt.
> Herrscher, durch deine Macht triumphirte der Römer und beugte
> Seinem Scepter die Welt, die du für deinen bestimmt.
> Freilich warst du ein heidnisher Gott, und glichest den Menschen,
> Doch die Menschen dafür glichen dem Göttergeschlecht.[20]

Here is a poet not merely dreaming among the ruins but writing
with life and energy that rivals that of a contemporary of the
great events such as Horace.

Waiblinger, as nearly every traveller before him, found at
once that the most obvious characteristic of Italy was the remains of ancient Rome; but he sought to give to his German
readers an original and individualistic impression of Roman
antiquity. He neither annotated his works with dry citations
from Lucan and Silius Italicus in the fashion of Addison nor
bored his readers with melancholy laments on the fallen glory of
Rome in the manner of the romanticists. Breaking with these
worn-out conventions, he made his material as realistic as possible. His explorations of Pompeii and the descriptions of the
ancient city are scientifically accurate and yet done with an effectiveness that would do credit to a trained archaeologist. Elsewhere when he described ancient monuments he tried to give us
a picture of them in their greatest magnificence. His lines on the
temple of Jupiter Stator contain no obscure urge to be a "pagan
suckled on a creed outworn" but rather a beautiful tribute to the
spirit that motivated the Peace of Augustus. Waiblinger occas-

---

19. *Gedichte aus Italien,* II, 81.
20. *Ibid.,* p. 82.

ionally fell into the tiresome style of gloomy romanticists pining
among the ruins, but the work of his last years shows none of
this and is characterized by a new orientation toward a person-
alized style and care in executing his purpose of untangling
the remaining threads of antiquity that he found in Italy for his
German readers.

* * * * * * * * * *

For several reasons we must consider Waiblinger's treatment
of Greek and of Roman antiquity under different headings. In
the first place, ancient Italy saw the two nations flourish side by
side, and Magna Graecia was as distinct from central Italy and
Rome as Rome herself was from the Celtic north. In the second
place, since the middle of the eighteenth century modern scholarship has carefully distinguished Greek and Roman cultural traditions, a distinction to be found in Waiblinger's own works even
before he went to Italy.[21] The young author of *Phaethon* composed works with such suggestive titles as *Lieder der Griechen* and
Vier Erzählungen aus der Geschichte des jetzigen Griechenlands
under the influence of his master, Hölderlin; and Gustav Schwab
spurred him on to read Xenophon, Homer, the *Batrachomyoma-
chia*, Lysias, Isocrates, Plutarch, Sophocles, Euripides, and Anacreon.[22] In the poet's early diaries the pages are filled with
quotations from Greek authors, and his phrase "die Alten" was
practically synonymous with "die Griechen". When he went to
Italy, he could not help but observe the distinctive qualities of
Greek art in the museums.

Waiblinger was almost as well versed in Greek literature as
he was in Latin. The diaries show numerous comments on Greek
authors, quotations from them, and discussions of ideas taken
immediately from Greek classics. Among other things, we have
a short summary of Plato's *Symposium*, and accompanying this
entry are his own "Aphorismen über die Liebe" in which he presents such concepts as that of "eine edlere und eine unedlere
Liebe."[23] In other passages he speaks of favorite philosophical
ideas and literary works adopted from Greek literature.

Although Rome was the material fulfillment of Waiblinger's
ideal of the south, the most important formative influence on

---

21. For a careful distinction between Greek and Roman influence on
Germany see the introduction to Butler.
22. Frey, p. 46 *et seq.*
23. *Werke.* IV, 240.

him in creating this ideal was not so much the ideology of modern writers as Waiblinger's own study of Greek literature and art. Waiblinger's early work, for example, the *Erzählungen aus der Geschichte des jetzigen Griechenlands,* like Goethe's "Land der Citronen und Goldorangen," is basically the product of an indefinite yearning for the south. It was only after Waiblinger arrived in Italy and saw the splendid remains of the lands of Magna Graecia that he was able to formulate his ideas on Greek culture.

In exploring the remains of ancient Greece in Italy Waiblinger followed Winckelmann's methods. Just as Winckelmann had worked quietly in the Roman museums and made occasional trips to southern Italy to visit Greek ruins, so Waiblinger organized his program. Most of Waiblinger's comments on Greek art are based almost exclusively on his experiences in Sicily and in Roman museums.

Among Waiblinger's earliest exercises were essays on Greek art. It is difficult to estimate the degree of originality he attained, since he undoubtedly adopted uncritically many ideas that were current in the Stuttgart group surrounding the Boisserées and Dannecker. Nevertheless, many entries in his diary from this period show a fine appreciation of what little he had gleaned about the masterpieces of Greek art without ever having seen them.[24] He had a broad knowledge of Greek sculpture, and in Rome he increased it by haunting the museums. However, in Italy there was a change. He was no longer so interested in aesthetic theory as in the interpretation of the art of the ancients as a part of his entire picture of Italy. His lines on the Venus di Milo give us his conception of the idealism of Greek art:

> Menschen steigen zum Himmel: zur schönen olympischen Blume
> Schliesset der irdische Keim drüben im Lichte sich auf.
> Geist verschmilzt sich mit Geist, und im freier entfalteten Leben
> Wird die sterbliche Form schöner und heil'ger verklärt.[25]

The Venus of the Capitol appears in a quite different light as the representative of all the sensual tendencies of antiquity, a sensualism that Waiblinger felt was closely related to the nature of the southern peoples:

> Götter steigen herab in menschliche Hülle sich bergend,
> Und dem Sterblichen mischt gern sich das Himmlische bei.
> Sinnlicher Fülle hast du, uranische geistige Schönheit,

---

24. *E.g., Werke,* IV, 224-226.
25. *Gedichte aus Italien,* II, 48.

All' dein Wesen und Sein, all' dein Geheimniss vertraut.
Weib ist die Göttin, vergängliche Form hat das Ew'ge gewählet,
Aber das Sinnliche wirkt auch auf das Sinnliche nur.[26]

However, the clarity and beauty of the Greek spirit transcended everything else for Waiblinger. The Venus who rose from the blue Mediterranean and shed her radiant beauty over all antiquity resembled the Venus di Milo in her highest qualities. He wrote of the Venus dei Medici:

Nie ist die Göttin geworden, von Anfang ist sie, vollkommen
Stieg sie der Welt aus des Meers rauschenden Wassern empor.
In der flüchtigen Natur ist sie die dauernde Seele,
Und im Wechsel der Form ist sie das ew'ge Gesetz,
Unter sichtbar Gemischtem die tief unsichtbare Einheit,
Unter dem Einzelnen ruht bleibend als Ganzes sie fest.
Und also vollkommne Idee gereifter dauernder Schönheit
Zeigt sie dem Sinn nicht, dem Geist nur die olympische Macht.[27]

An age of fable surrounded these remarkable works of art for Waiblinger, and he felt that the fable giving the theme to many pieces was as pure and beautiful in its conception as the representation in stone, for example, the Niobe legend as conceived by Scopas in his group now in Florence.[28]

Roman antiquity could offer Waiblinger no such outstanding monuments of art which interpreted the soul of a highly gifted people. The remains of ancient Rome had given him an idea of the private life and character of the conquerors of the world. In Sicily Waiblinger learned about Greek history and Greek daily life, for on that island the culture of ancient Greece had transplanted itself completely. Waiblinger's "Oden und Elegien aus Sicilien" consist of a series of poems on Sicilian antiquities and Sicilian landscape, and there are pieces on such suggestive themes as Syracuse, Timoleon, and Girgenti as well as on the natural beauties of Sicily.

When Waiblinger first sailed into Syracuse, he must have thought of the chaotic political history of the island, plagued by tyrants and the Athenian wars and Roman conquerors. He opened this series of odes with a fearful picture of the raging Marcellus destroying Syracuse, but at the same time he recalled that the Greeks had given Sicily a tradition that continues to reflect the bright genius of the Hellenistic peoples.[29] The poet gave an account of the positive accomplishments of the Greeks in Sicily

---

26. *Ibid.*
27. *Ibid.*, p. 49.
28. *Ibid.*, p. 139.
29. *Ibid.*, p. 139-141.

and did not repeat the turbulent political history of the island. He tarried at the villa of Timoleon and composed verses to glorify the political idealism of the liberator of Sicily; and at Girgenti the ruins of the ancient temple baking in the hot Sicilian sun brought to his mind's eye an image of the colorful religious ceremony of the ancients, of all the beauty of formal Greek religion.[30]

These brilliant pictures of Greek life and legend show a remarkable imagination able to create brilliant pictures of a dead civilization from modern ruins. Just as Waiblinger felt that he saw classic faces and figures in modern Italian women and Virgilian landscape in the valleys and hills of Latium, so also he found the magic of Greek life enduring in the atmosphere of Sicily. Indeed, he almost carried this notion to an unreasonable extreme, for he never mentioned Sicilian squalor so repulsive to most northern Europeans. Like Washington Irving, who ignored the industrial revolution in England to hunt down every trace of old English life, Waiblinger, undisturbed by the pitiful aspect of the modern Sicilian, thought in terms of the wealthy, luxuriant granary of the ancient world.

Waiblinger's neo-hellenism did not come to full flower as Byron's did, but in Italy his Greek studies never flagged, and he was able to put them to good use. If Rome failed to bring forth the ideal of beauty that Waiblinger and most other travellers have felt to be native to southern lands, it was not lacking in other parts of Italy, for Greek culture had penetrated thoroughly the life of the peninsula. Thus Waiblinger was able to show that Italy preserved relics of Greek as well as Roman culture and that Italy alone could fulfill the thirst of the northerner for the glories of ancient civilization.

---

30. *Ibid.*, p. 144.

CHAPTER VII

WAIBLINGER AND THE RENAISSANCE

Of all the ages when Italy has been a vital cultural factor in the evolution of western Europe, the period of the Renaissance stands out above all others. Not only is the Italian Renaissance the age which left the most pronounced effects on the national character of Italy herself, but it is also the one great movement without which our modern age would never have come into existence. Waiblinger's works dealing with Italy are filled with reminiscences of the Italy of the fourteenth, fifteenth, and sixteenth centuries; but during the sixteenth and seventeenth centuries, writers on Italy and travellers in the country had been too interested in their decadent Italian contemporaries to pay due tribute to the masters of literature and the arts in the Renaissance;[1] and it was only in the latter half of the eighteenth century that there was some genuine appreciation of the best in the Italian Renaissance. It is not surprising that the first important estimates of the Renaissance came from the incipient romanticism of Germany, the country where romanticism signified universality. Karl Philipp Moritz, best known as the author of *Anton Reiser,* was in Italy at the time Goethe was there, and he had earnestly tried to enter into the spirit of the Renaissance, although he was somewhat deficient in historical perspective. A half a dozen years earlier Wilhelm Heinse's *Ardinghello* with its emphasis on "aesthetic immoralism" had been widely read. Heinse, like his hero, had been an enthusiastic admirer of the ideal of the "Renaissance gentleman," and actually he was able to understand the Renaissance considerably more effectively than the modest and often purblind plodder Moritz.

Even more important was Goethe with his fine evaluation of the Renaissance in the diaries and his *Italienische Reise,* in which he shows an appreciation of the masters of Renaissance art that can only come from a kindred spirit. His translation of Benvenuto Cellini's *Autobiography* (1803) is especially significant, for he gave to the German people through this translation a characteristic work of the period. The note struck by this work

---

1. Von Klenze, p. 10.

was taken up at once by the early romanticists, who demanded
universality in life and art; and during the first years of the
nineteenth century there was a flood of critical and historical
material on all periods of the Italian Renaissance from the
Schlegels, Tieck, and others.

While the immediate background of Waiblinger's interest in
the Renaissance comes from the German literary tradition and
from his own environment during his sojourn in Italy, it is interesting to observe the growth of English interest in the Italian
Renaissance during the eighteenth and early nineteenth centuries. Waiblinger read English well, and he was undoubtedly impressed by many of Byron's glowing descriptions of Renaissance
Italy. Marshall's study of Anglo-Italian literary relations just
before the flowering of English romanticism traces the interest
in the Italian Renaissance in England from 1755 to 1815. During
the eighties, at the time when Heinse, Moritz, and Goethe began
to intensify German interest in Italy, a similar rehabilitation of
Italy took place in England, particularly evident in Sir Joshua
Reynolds' interest in Italian Renaissance painters and in Hester
Lynch Thrale Piozzi's encouragement of the study of Italian
literature.   By the beginning of the second decade of the nineteenth century Leigh Hunt, Walter Savage Landor, Byron and
others had paved the way for a new tradition of Anglo-Italian
literary relations that was to last through D. G. Rosetti and J. A.
Symonds down to our own day. The German poet may well have
been influenced by English writers other than Byron in the
course of his wide reading.

This parallelism between developments in England and Waiblinger's interests is even more obvious in *Liebe und Hass,* written when he was seventeen years old. Fauconnet has pointed out
the similarity with such works as *Emilia Galotti* and *Fiesco* in
the treatment of the Renaissance background.[2] This use of a
Renaissance setting is also characteristic of some of the sensational books by Horace Walpole, Ann Radcliffe, and "Monk"
Lewis. Neither the Englishmen nor Waiblinger made any contribution to a proper understanding of the Renaissance in these
works. Waiblinger was destined to have a true concept of the
Renaissance only after he extended his reading beyond the

---

2. *Liebe und Hass* (1914), p. iv-v.

Gothic novels and actually saw the heritage of the Renaissance in Italy.

Undoubtedly the greatest and most important accomplishments of the Renaissance in Italy lie in the field of the arts. In this respect Italy was particularly important for Waiblinger, for he (like John Addington Symonds) realized that art was the "spiritual oxygen" on which the Renaissance man flourished. Every vestige of Renaissance art was important for him. An altar in a monastery in the hills pleased him as much as the great masterpieces of the Vatican. On the whole, however, he limits his comment on the art of the Renaissance to the more important masters, to those representative spirits who have come to be identified with the age. Most of Waiblinger's criticism is surprisingly close to standard modern opinions, and unquestionably he made his contribution toward the crystallization of modern ideas on Italian Renaissance art .

Waiblinger's comment on Raphael's *Stanzi* reveals that he was able to perceive clearly the truism of modern art histories that Raphael is the harmonist of classical and Christian traditions in the arts. A splendid characterization of Raphael's art is in the little epigram on the "Madonna del Gran Duca," an unusually fine portrayal of the spiritual and human values in the same piece:

Wie voll Unschuld du bist, du süss jungfräuliches Antlitz,
  So befangen, so sanft, kaum noch der Kindheit entblüht.
Schüchtern noch thust du, obwohl schon Mutter geworden, so bist du
  Dir's nicht bewusst, und weisst selbst noch nicht, wie dir geschah.[3]

Likewise Waiblinger perceived clearly the point of distinction between the two great painters of the Renaissance when he spoke of "sanfter Raffael und harter Michelangelo."[4] And just as we have seen the expansion of the adjective applied to the former, also we have a fine insight into the essential nature of the genius of Michelangelo:

Deiner Brust hat die güt'ge Natur nicht den Frieden gegeben,
  Der, wie der Frühling so zart, alles erheiternd verjüngt.
Du verschmähest den sanften Verkehr mit dem Genius, zürnend
  Stürmest, Titanen gleich, du in den Himmel empor.[5]

To what extent such observations as these two on Raphael and Michelangelo were original with Waiblinger cannot easily be

---

3. *Gedichte aus Italien*, II, 54.
4. *Werke*, II, 149.
5. *Gedichte aus Italien*, II, 54.

determined. Frequently he mentioned Giorgio Vasari's *Lives of the Painters*, but this work is chiefly valuable as a contemporary record rather than as advanced criticism. To be sure, many of Waiblinger's comments on Renaissance art were not entirely new, as, for example, his epigram on Titian's Venus:

> Das ist Venus, die Göttin, die hohe olympische Schönheit?
> Nicht die Venus ist das, aber der Venus Geschöpf.[6]

This comment is almost exactly the idea expressed some fifty years previously by Heinse in one of his travel essays,[7] but we have no proof that Waiblinger took it from Heinse or even knew it at all. The important evidence for Waiblinger's originality is that his observations on the art of the Renaissance showed a remarkable degree of consistency and accuracy in an age when the history of art had not yet fully developed as a scholarly discipline. Even more important is the ease with which Waiblinger seems to have entered into the spirit of the Renaissance. His lines on Benvenuto Cellini, quoted in Chapter II,[8] show a remarkable insight into the man's personality and art. Similar understanding is revealed in the first two lines of the epigram on Filippo Bruneleschi, the reformer of architecture in the first half of the fifteenth century:

> Herrliche Zeiten, da einst in geselligem Bunde die Künste
> Sich in Einem zum Werk Aller so thätig vereint![9]

Waiblinger found in Renaissance art the typical expression of the genius of the age; and whether or not his own thoughts on the subject were original, they represented a sympathetic approach and an effective interpretation for his German readers.

No less significant is Waiblinger's feeling for the literature of the Renaissance, but his remarks here are not as extensive as we might expect. He was strongly attracted to Ariosto, who represented for him at once a zest for life so typical of his age and an imaginative quality that surpassed that of his contemporaries. Waiblinger displayed much of the same enthusiasm for Ariosto that we find in that curious eighteenth century Englishman, William Huggins, who sought to acclimate the Italian poet to the north. Huggins, and later Waiblinger, found "satirical strokes of the sharpest poignancy, or poetical images of the sublimest in-

---

6. *Ibid.*
7. Heinse, *Werke*, VIII, 143.
8. *Gedichte aus Italien*, II, 54.
9. *Ibid.*

vention."[10] In Torquato Tasso Waiblinger found the beginning of a baroque tradition under which original genius had little chance:

> Du wirst bleiben, so lange Musik und melodischer Wohllaut
>   Dein entzückendes Welsch noch sich zur Wiege bestimmt,
> Und so lange die Lieb' in zärtlichem Feuer die Sprache
>   Der Musik, und des Reichs lieblicher Töne sich wählt.
> Aber Homer, er gefällt mir schon nicht im Virgil, wie gefiele
>   Darum in deinem Gedicht, Tasso, mir gar nun Virgil?[11]

In addition to Ariosto, Waiblinger also admired Petrarch and Boccaccio as representatives of the Italian Renaissance.[12] He saw in Petrarch the *archipoeta* of love interpreted in a new manner,[13] and in Boccaccio he saw the prime example of the great artist who maintained a healthy realism as an integral element of his art.[14] It is unfortunate that Waiblinger did not have more to say about the literature of the Italian Renaissance; but, just as in the case of art, he was more interested in catching the spirit of the age than in the details of scholarship.

Waiblinger's interest in the Italian Renaissance comes into sharp focus in *Das Blumenfest*. It is an inferior tale composed mainly to fill space in the *Almanach auf das Jahr 1829*, but the sixteenth century setting lends it some value as a historical romance. Waiblinger attempted to create the atmosphere of the Renaissance through typical scenes, characters, and situations of the period; but sometimes these characters seem to be closer to the pulp literature of Waiblinger's day than to accurate historical portrayal. The endless series of intrigues, treachery, and counter-plots might be characteristic of the Italian Renaissance, but they were even more characteristic of cheap novels of the late eighteenth and early nineteenth centuries. The same holds true for the stock characters of the proud, aristocratic old prince and his dashing son, the young Prince Chigi, and all the voluptuous Italian women who appear in the story. Of more abiding interest are the scenes which attempt to give a picture of manners and daily life in the sixteenth century. For example, the description of the religious procession during the festival of flowers at Genzano illustrates how Waiblinger visualized the worldly re-

---

10. *Apud* Marshall, p. 33.
11. *Gedichte aus Italien*, II, 64.
12. However, neither author ever attained the importance of Ariosto for him. *Cf.* Friedrich, p. 328.
13. *Gedichte aus Italien*, II, 62.
14. *Ibid.*, p. 63.

ligion of the period.[15] Again we find a colorful account of Genzano decorated for a Renaissance festival:

> Unterdessen hatte man schon die Strasse, die zum Altar und zur Kirche hinaufführte, über und über mit Blumen bedeckt. In die verschiedenartigsten Bilder hatte man die Flora geformt; hier bemerkte man einen Tempel von weissen Blumen auf grünem Myrtengrunde, auf dessen Altar eine Flamme von Purpurrosen brannte; dort schoben sich liebliche Arabesken durcheinander, architektonische Zierrathen, so niedlich, als man es nur mit der leicht verwehenden Fülle von so zarten Blättern zu Stande bringen konnte. An manchen Orten sah man die Wappen des Hauses auf die Laubfläche gezeichnet und mit Blumen gemalt; dann gewahrte man wieder Säulen und kleine Obelisken mit Inschriften, Gärten mit artigen Lusthäusern, Altäre, Kirchen, menschliche Figuren, Amorinen, Engelchen, phantastische geflügelte Thiere, Tauben und anderes hübsches Geflügel, das Alles die Länge der Strasse hin mit der sinnreichen Auswahl von Farben und Blättern geziert war, und das Bild der heiligen Mutter der allgemeinen Verehrung darbot.[16]

Thus Waiblinger envisaged the genius of the age of Renaissance with its tradition of display and pageantry, inherited in part from the middle ages, but arranging the whole with a fine artistic sense.

Waiblinger did not make a thorough investigation of the Renaissance comparable to the great works of Symonds and Burckhardt, but everywhere in his writings there are traces of his appreciation of this greatest period in Italian history. None of Waiblinger's works is devoted to a special consideration of the Renaissance, but the poet felt the inescapable influence of the Renaissance, and his work is replete with notes and observations on the period. Waiblinger wanted to enter into the spirit of the age so that he might look at it as a high water mark of history. In considering the arts and the literature of the period he sought characteristic figures such as Benvenuto Cellini and Ariosto, men who might not have lived and created so successfully in any other age. In addition, Waiblinger portrayed in broad outline the life of the Renaissance as a background of one of his stories, and here he followed the tradition of the romantic novelists such as Arnim and Hauff. Thus we not only have in Waiblinger's works a sympathetic interpretation of the Renaissance, but in one case an effort to recreate the life and manners of the Renaissance. However inexact some of Waiblinger's work may be by modern criteria, he showed much insight into the age and was generally objective.

---

15. *Werke*, III, 98.
16. *Ibid.*, p. 97.

CHAPTER VIII

WAIBLINGER AND CATHOLICISM

The predominance of the Roman Catholic religion in Italy is one of the hallmarks of the country. Not only in Rome but also all over Italy the externals of the Church are as much in evidence as in any other country of the world. Some prominent figures, for example Zacharias Werner and Friedrich (Maler) Müller, were even converted to the Italian variety of Catholicism in Waiblinger's own day. A classic expression of the attraction of Rome for men of the age is the famous speech of Mortimer Paulet in Schiller's *Maria Stuart* (lines 409-450). Driven by similar impulses, other northern Europeans accepted the Catholic faith during the reorientation toward Rome at the beginning of the last century. Much of the success of the Church might be attributed to the violent reaction against the Voltairean motto of "Écrasez l'infâme" and against other vestiges of rationalism; but when Waiblinger began to write, this movement had practically spent itself in Germany. Ultramontanism had retreated to the studies of Brentano and Görres, and in literature there was a movement toward a new synthesis of rationalism and romanticism and thereby a more objective attitude toward the Church of Rome.

Although Waiblinger never renounced his Protestant faith there is strong evidence of a passion for Catholicism not unlike that which attracted Novalis.[1] Waiblinger's own religious background had been strictly Protestant, and he had at one time even been a seminary student. At Tübingen, however, he gradually moved away from the fundamentalist variety of Protestantism under the influence of such men as Mörike and Ludwig Bauer. He fell in with the spirit of the times and began to entertain a healthy tolerance for all religions. *Phaethon* reveals a neopaganism reminiscent of Hölderlin and André Chénier; and the diaries from this period are full of excerpts from Novalis and Görres.[2] When Waiblinger went to Italy, he was prepared to view Catholicism objectively as a national religion of a country where he was a guest.

In Italy Waiblinger sensed a distinctly religious atmosphere that is obvious to any observant tourist. Where else but Rome

1. *Cf.* Friedrich, p. 66, 78.
2. Frey, p. 64.

could one hear "der Abendglocken tausendstimmig Geläut,³ and
where else but in the calm peace of a monastery in the Italian
hills could one speak so feelingly of "Des Klosters stiller Garten
und Blumenweg"?⁴ No other Catholic country, not even Spain,
can show the pontifical glory of Rome flourishing side by side
with a simple folk religion that pervades the entire country. In
Rome Waiblinger became acquainted with all the public and
private functions of the Roman See; and during his travels
through the Sabine country, Latium, and the south he came into
contact with the religion of the peasants. Waiblinger saw all aspects of the religious life of the country — the princes of the
Church in Rome, the humble but sometimes worldly country
priest, the riotous celebration of the carnival; and he properly
concluded that in Italy the national religion had permeated
every part of the life of the people, seven days a week, for better
or for worse.⁵

Waiblinger saw that the Catholic religion reflected not only
the manners and daily life of the people, but also a thousand
years of Italian history. He felt strongly about the political
domination of Italy by the pope, especially in connection with the
mediaeval struggles between the popes and the German emperors. Of Friedrich II he wrote:

> Dein Feind, o Friedrich? Grössern bekämpfte nie
> Ein Held, sei's denn der Engel des Schwerts vielleicht,
> Der Belial schlug. O Staub des Herrschers,
> Betet' ich Irdisches an, du wärst es.⁶

In the nineteenth century the German imperial dream of dominating Italy lay peacefully with the ashes of the Hohenstaufen
and remained a mere historical memory. Still Waiblinger had the
most profound respect for the enduring contribution of the
Church as an inspiration to artists, and he wrote of the great
work of Michelangelo in the Vatican in glowing terms:

> Also thürmt' er die Kuppel der Basilik' in die Lüfte,
> Schuf er den Moses, und so selber den Heiland der Welt.
> Also malt' er das jüngst Gericht und die grossen Propheten,
> Um, wie kein Sterblicher je, dreifach unsterblich zu sein.⁷

Even if the Church had lost its political power, its powerful appeal to the people and its importance as a social force was no less

---

3. *Gedichte aus Italien*, II, 27.
4. *Ibid.*, p. 146.
5. *Cf. Werke*, VIII, 231.
6. *Gedichte aus Italien*, II, 147.
7. *Ibid.*, p. 55-56.

significant, a point that Waiblinger made in the opening lines of his fragment, "Die Nacht in St. Peter."[8]

Of all the material manifestations of the Church, the personnel of the Church impressed Waiblinger most. He was attracted by the hordes of priests and monks who seemed to him to make up a fourth of the total population of Italy[9] and by the quiet and persistent manner in which they pursued their calling. He wrote of no scheming cardinals and inordinately ambitious princes of the church but rather of humble priests with no ambitions for secular or ecclesiastical distinction. Waiblinger sought in Italy the type of priest that he had known in the simple pastorates of his Swabian home, unassuming and yet eager to fulfill their mission on earth, for example, the *piferari*.

In Olevano Waiblinger stayed at the home of a typical country priest. He was a poor but sincere man and quite proud of his little bit of learning, which Waiblinger gently satirized.[10] Again at Albano he stayed with a priest and reproached himself for having chosen the career of a wanderer and sacrificed similar happiness that he might have known in a German parsonage.[11] In Palestrina he appreciated the human qualities of the local abbot, who seemed to Waiblinger to be "ein wenig Libertin";[12] and the two men got along famously when Waiblinger became aware of the soundness of the man's learning and his modesty in concealing it. Waiblinger's fundamentally genial personality came out in his description of an insane Capuchin monk who peddled crosses over the countryside and would have his customers kiss his own cross which he claimed to be from the original. The poet did his bidding and replied to his speech with a jovial but faintly ironical answer.[13] Waiblinger found the Italian clerics to be a familiar group in Italian society, and he treated them with the same broad tolerance with which he dealt with other classes of Italians.

Although Waiblinger always maintained a feeling of superiority over the average man, he thought of his own educational advantages merely as an accident of birth and environment.[14]

---

8. *Ibid.*, p. 94.
9. *Werke*, VIII, 149.
10. *Ibid.*, p. 147.
11. *Ibid.*, p. 182-183.
12. *Ibid.*, p. 241.
13. *Ibid.*, p. 157.
14. Rapp, p. 257.

Accordingly Waiblinger was able to retain a generous but critical attitude toward his fellow men. Such was the case with religious ceremony and art, which Waiblinger recognized as externals but at the same time essential for the continuity of the institution. He was fully aware of the Church's policy of promoting pomp and ceremony as a device to encourage solidarity, for he observed on more than one occasion how a religious festival attracted crowds from far and near, regardless of whether all were communicants. He admitted simply, "So kam auch ich mit ihnen," for, like a simple hill priest, he too was overawed by the magificent ritual at St. Peter's. He appreciated fully a work of art inspired by pure religious sentiment, but at the same time he denounced bad taste in religious art without reservation. He described the Madonna di Foligno with utmost admiration:

> In den Himmel erhaben, zur Königin herrlich verkläret,
>> Blieb dir das Herz, wie es war, aber es wuchs dir der Geist.
> Denn man betet dich an, du umgiebst dich mit strahlender Hoheit,
>> Und der Vater hat dir längst dein Geheimniss enthüllt.[15]

But contrasting with these verses of admiration, he summoned all the venom of an irascible critic in condemning the tasteless version of the crucifixion by Guido Reni and the monstrous scene of the tortures of the saints by Nicolas Poussin:

> Nein, dass nenn' ich Tortur, das ist eine Strafe, so schrecklich,
>> Dass sie der Maler allein, der sie gebildet, verdient.[16]

Waiblinger's criticism is subjective, but it is to the point and effective.

Waiblinger's description of the Roman holidays occasioned by church ceremonies echo plainly the *panem et circenses* characteristic of Juvenal's pictures of pagan festivities, for he saw how the Roman mob congregated as eagerly to see the pope and all his splendor as they did to greet a conqueror returning to distribute grain and stage great public circuses. In the passages of *Das Blumenfest* describing the baptism of the Turkish lady Zuleika we have a cross-section of the mob gathered for the solemnity and brilliance of the papal ceremonies.[17] Waiblinger described the entire ceremony, with the exception of certain passages intimately connected with the plot, with the straightforward manner of a Sabine peasant who had come to town for the brilliant occasion.

---

15. *Gedichte aus Italien*, II, 54.
16. *Ibid.*, p. 74.
17. *Werke*, III, 125-127.

In more refined language and avoiding the garish tone of his
descriptions of great papal holidays, Waiblinger often portrayed
the lesser functions of the Church as a medium of communica-
tion between God and the individual. In the short elegy "Ora
pro nobis" he could reveal the purest religious sentiment:

> Heil'ge Dämmrung waltet durch der Rotunda
> Tausendjähr'ge Wölbung, der Geist des Abends
> Mahnt zum Beten, mahnet zur letzten Andacht,
> Ora pro nobis.
>
> Auf den Knieen umher in des Tempels hoher
> Rundung liegt das gläubige Volk, und Alles
> Tönt einstimmig, Jungfrau, dein Lob und flehet:
> Ora pro nobis.[18]

Waiblinger appreciated this aspect of the Church more than any
other, for here he found a genuineness of emotion that is miss-
ing in the great spectacles.

Nevertheless, Waiblinger felt that the sensational processions
and celebrations were more characteristic of the Church than
the unassuming worship of individuals. In the middle of his
fragmentary "Die Nacht in St. Peter," a poem intended to illustrate his personal religion, he broke out with a colorful description of celestial courtiers, baroque in the brilliance of externals
and Swedenborgian in expanse of imagination. Quickly, however, he recalled the tone of his poem, waved aside the heirs of
St. Peter with a scornful, "Sie alle sitzen stumm in ihrem Gold,"
and described the contrasting qualities of Christ in a simpler
note.[19] Yet in spite of this feeling for the simple religion that
Waiblinger always cherished, we know that his chief pleasures
came from carousals at carnival time, the most worldly of all the
secular functions of the Church. Here, as usual, we find Waiblinger projecting himself into the character of the Italian people who knew nothing of the stern admonitions of Protestant
ministers about a "Sunday religion."

If religious ceremony appealed to Waiblinger as an outlet
for the emotions of the people, then religious art appealed to him
all the more as the highest expression of the creative artist. In
the greatest works of religious art he found the purest and most
beautiful sentiment transposed into enduring form by gifted
men, from the primitives whose naïve madonnas impart a feeling of absolute trust in God to the artists of the Renaissance who

18. *Gedichte aus Italien*, II, 33.
19. *Ibid.*, p. 102-103.

glorified the power and the pomp of the papacy. He had the highest praise for Raphael's work in the Vatican;[20] but Fra Giovanni
da Fiesole did not suffer by comparison, for his expression of
his convictions have their own beauty.[21] Waiblinger admired any
art that revealed purity of thought and sincerity of purpose.

Nor did Waiblinger confine his comments on ecclesiastical
art to the Roman scene, for he found that every village chapel
might offer something of interest. A monastery at Licenza, not
far from the villa of Horace, revealed a distinguished structure
combined with a landscape impossible at Rome.[22] At Civitella
Waiblinger marvelled at the "wunderbare Einfältigkeit" of the
local Franciscan monastery,[23] and at Torre dell 'Annunziata near
Vesuvius he discovered a wayside chapel distinguished by a "herrliche Säulenreihe in kleinem Maasse."[24] In the country churches
and homes of religious communities Waiblinger found a simple
architectural style whose homely beauty was greatly enhanced
by the landscape, and this he found to be a pleasing contrast to
the brilliance of Rome.

But this aspect of religious art, like the simpler religious ceremonies, did not excite his interest to the degree which he reserved for the great palaces of the Church in Rome. He was properly
impressed with the colossal, the spectacular, and the famous.
Eduard, the young German in *Die heilige Woche*, possibly a par-
tial self-portrait of the writer, stood in awe of the enormous art
treasures amassed in the Vatican and reacted appropriately.[25]

Waiblinger was not the man to take his religion too seriously,
but he maintained the utmost tolerance toward Catholic Italy
and tact in dealing with clerics and the more devout communicants. He showed a deep respect for religious sincerity, even if
he himself had no profound convictions. For this reason he was
able to maintain a certain objectivity in describing the functions
and achievements of the Church in Italy. He realized that the
Catholic faith was more deeply rooted in Italy than in any other
European country, and therefore he felt that it was necessary to
give due attention to its most obvious characteristics in order to
give a complete picture of Italy to his German readers. Natural-

20. *Ibid.*, p. 53.
21. *Ibid.*, p. 51.
22. *Werke*, VIII, 114.
23. *Werke*, IX, 99.
24. *Ibid.*, p. 213.
25. *Werke*, IV, 64-65.

ly, he dwelt for the most part on ecclesiastical ceremony and art, the two aspects of the Church in Italy that impress the traveller most; and he discussed the most colorful and grandiose ceremonies and the most famous works of art. He wove these notes into his work with such skill that he has given us the proper comprehension of the omnipresence of the Church in Italian life.

CHAPTER IX

CONCLUSION

Our investigation of Waiblinger's Italian experience has led
us through nearly all the salient features of Italy, both as he saw
it in the early nineteenth century and as he interpreted its brilliant history. At this point it is appropriate to recapitulate and
coordinate the evidence in order to show at a glance the significance of Italy for Waiblinger and in turn the significance of his
work in the general literary tradition of Germany and Europe.

In the first chapter we noted how Italy represented for Waiblinger a kind of a promised land; and, when he was casting
about as a young man who had suffered several misfortunes, not
the least of which was his failure to become well-known in literary circles at home, the opportunity to go to Italy came as a
happy wind-fall for him. After the first few months in Italy he
realized that he had discovered his true mission in life. He began
to look upon Italy as his real home, the country of his heart's
desire; and he envisioned his life's task as revealing the glories
of Italy to his less fortunate countrymen.

Waiblinger's Italian work shows superiority over his earlier
publications in style and in content; but we are mainly interested
in content, since he was more of an interpreter than a strictly
creative artist. The early drama *Liebe und Hass*, although set in
Italy, leaves us with an extremely vague conception of the characters and their environment due to the faulty style and construc-
tion of the play. In contrast with the Italian travel sketches this
early drama appears in an even more unfavorable light. The
early work is all built on themes with which the poet was un-
familiar and was shaped in the form of purely imaginative work,
but in Italy Waiblinger was able to observe life and record his
reactions objectively. His major work in Italy was poetry on
Italian themes, travel sketches, and short stories, the latter being
of inferior quality because he tended to lose sight of the reality
with which he was familiar. Receptive to everything that he
saw, Waiblinger's fairness to all aspects of Italy, past and present, is characteristic of his work. An unprejudiced attitude was
a necessary prerequisite to an accurate account of Italy, and

Waiblinger discovered it as an automatic virtue, a by-product of his enthusiastic approach.

He was interested not merely in the cultural life of Italy, but also in her people, popular traditions, and natural beauties. Winckelmann had been exclusively interested in art. Goethe's interests in Italy were intimately associated with the spiritual rejuvenation that he underwent, and he did not go into the great detail that Waiblinger did in writing about Italy. Waiblinger enjoyed the advantage of understanding the concept of a nation as the product of a totality of forces. To Mme. de Staël Germany was the land of Weimar classicism, but her friend August Wilhelm Schlegel looked upon his native land as the product of centuries of traditions, both literary and popular, of a people with distinct racial characteristics, of a landscape familiar as home, of a distinct religion. Waiblinger had a similar attitude toward Italy as a part of his romantic heritage; and his unsystematic presentation makes it none the less valuable, for his work is readable and may well have made at least as great an impression on the popular mind of Germany as the work of more scholarly romanticists.

It matters little whether Waiblinger was a thoroughly sound critic in matters requiring taste and artistic perception, although he ordinarily displayed a fine sense of values. The importance of his work lies rather in his general orientation. Just as travellers of the sixteenth, seventeenth, and eighteenth centuries had been inspired with the love of antiquity by the Renaissance and sought nothing else in Italy, so we may expect a new and different orientation toward Italy following the romantic upheaval. In Waiblinger's work we have a body of writings dealing exclusively with Italy and written by a man who spent the most fruitful years of his life there. Here is not only a compendium of what the age thought and wrote about Italy but also the ideas of a man who was eminently qualified for the position of Italy's interpreter to Germany.

In the field of the arts we find that Waiblinger did not have a blind admiration of Raphael and his followers to the disadvantage of other Italian artists. Winckelmann had prepared the way for a thorough appreciation of the art of antiquity, and Waiblinger wandered through the villas and museums of Rome armed with the monumental *Geschichte der Kunst des Altertums*

and had as comprehensive an understanding as possible in his day
for the art of the ancients. Greek art was no longer simply another aspect of classical civilization but rather the work of artists comparable in their own right to the great figures of the
Italian Renaissance. Similarly, the art of the middle ages, almost
completely ignored up to the end of the eighteenth century, offered to Waiblinger works that are thoroughly justifiable as expressing the spirit of the age that produced them. Perhaps the
best evidence for Waiblinger's understanding in the fields of
painting, sculpture, and architecture is the record of his experience in Sicily, where ancient, Islamic, mediaeval Christian, and
Renaissance styles occur in motley confusion. Each is significant
for him in the light of the civilization that produced it.

Italian literature had undergone a wholesale re-evaluation
in the hands of the German romanticists; and Waiblinger, already acquainted with Italian literature during his German
period as we note in *Drei Tage in der Unterwelt,* was able to add
local color to his appreciation of Italian literature from his vant-
age point in the place of its origin. His remarks on the Italian
drama are particularly noteworthy. He contrasted the stiff
pseudo-classicism of Alfieri unfavorably with the merry operas
and folk plays of Metastasio and Goldoni, which seemed to him to
be more expressive of the national temperament. He found that
Mme. de Staël's Corinne was not a mere fiction but typical of
living people in Italy such as Rosa Taddei and the Cavaliere
Sgricci, whose improvisations represented a popular poetry of
equal merit with the folksongs rediscovered by the romanticists.

Of utmost importance is Waiblinger's appreciation of the
Italian landscape. To be sure, there were the same hills, valleys,
plains, and rivers that were described adequately enough by
Virgil and Horace; but most earlier travellers seem to have been
content with quoting the classics for any effect of Italian scenery that they wished to convey. Waiblinger, well schooled in ancient literatures, might have done the same; but his personal
affection for a scene such as the Bandusian Fountain was so profound that he described it in his own words, quoting Horace only
for the sake of comparison. In addition, he saw a landscape different from the one that the ancients knew because of the rise
and fall of the works of man. The Campo Vaccino was hardly the
busy Forum of antiquity, and the Appian Way certainly pre-

sented a different scene from the festive thoroughfare of Roman conquerors. Ostia was but a shadow of its former self:

> Einsam graut das Kastell in weiter schweigender Wildniss,
> Trümmer der mächtigen Stadt liegen wie Gräber umher.
> Einst umspülte sie Meer, nun zog sich's zurück, und die Erde
> Müssen wir jegliches Jahr feuchter und trockener sehn.[1]

Thus Waiblinger described Italy as the modern traveller would see it, still possessing the charm of antiquity, but modified by the hand of time.

His experience among the people has no parallel in the writings of other travellers in Italy. Before Waiblinger many visitors in Italy had considered the modern inhabitants to be degenerate heirs of the ancient Romans. The people were dirty, dishonest, illiterate, and completely unworthy of their ancestors. Waiblinger was not affected by these conventional attitudes, and he wrote about any Italian who was colorful or otherwise interesting. On the whole he found that the Italian people consisted of beautiful, sensuous women and extremely lazy men. Our modern popular conception of Italy as the land of *dolce far niente* checks closely with the idea that Waiblinger wanted to convey. However, Waiblinger did not dwell on this single superficial notion. He finds many individuals typical of the country and yet highly individualistic. Thus we are introduced to the bohemian painter in Rome, the kindly but ignorant country priest, the intoxicated *improvisatore*, the ex-bandit captain, and many others. Waiblinger found Italy rich not only in cultural traditions but also in the life of her people.

Ancillary to Waiblinger's love for the people was the fascination that the Catholic Church, dominant in Italy for over fifteen hundred years, had for him. He did not succumb to the spell of the Church as had certain German compatriots such as Friedrich (Maler) Müller, Zacharias Werner, Friedrich Schlegel, and Joseph Görres; but he did feel the attraction of ecclesiastical ceremony and art, a factor that impresses travellers from Protestant countries even today. He saw in the great cathedrals and religious paintings a genuine expression of the spirit of the people, and in this way he portrayed to his German readers one of the most striking aspects of Italy.

While Waiblinger understood quite well the cultural traditions of Italy, it was another matter to be able to identify the basic

---

1. *Gedichte aus Italien*, II, 48.

characteristics of the two great periods in her history, namely, classical antiquity and the Renaissance. Older travellers had, indeed, exploited classical antiquity, but they did not view it as one period in the development of a nation. Waiblinger was not only interested in ancient Rome for her own virtues but also for her influence on the life and civilization of modern Italy. Accordingly, he was able to make ancient Rome and Greece live as they never had in the works of earlier authors. He treated the Renaissance in much the same way, as a period that endowed modern Italy with a vitality and importance recognized by all Europe. Waiblinger knew and loved antiquity and Renaissance so well that he re-lived them, and it was his very enthusiasm that gave his work historical perspective.

These main points in this study represent a summary of Waiblinger's most important achievement in life. Other problems in his life and work are of minor importance in relation to the Italian experience and the content of his writings dealing with Italy. The problem of Waiblinger's subsequent influence is a difficult one. To what extent he influenced such men as Paul Heyse and Jacob Burckhardt would be difficult to ascertain without a careful analysis of the reading of these men. Beyond a few surmises the most that one can say is that Waiblinger's Italy is essentially the Italy that one finds in modern travel books, that no earlier writer presented his material with the same effectiveness, and that the similarity between Waiblinger's attitudes and the notions of other travellers and historians suggests that his writings entered into the mainstream of European thought.

BIBLIOGRAPHY[1]

I. *Editions of Waiblinger's Works*

Gesammelte Werke, mit des Dichters Leben von H. v. Canitz. Hamburg, Georg Heubel, 1839-1840. 9 v. Heubel published the second edition in nine volumes in 1842, and it has been used as the source for citations in this study. The second edition is identical with the first with the following exceptions: (1) The first edition contained only one engraving, the bust of Waiblinger by Wagner in the first volume; (2) two early poems and three passages from *Faust,* erroneously attributed to Waiblinger in the first edition, have been deleted and three new poems inserted in their place; (3) p. 241-276 of v. VI, which contained the "Lieder der Griechen," have been deleted from the second edition; and (4) the excerpt from *Laokoon* attributed to Waiblinger in v. IV has been removed. A third edition from the same plates as the 1842 edition was issued in Pforzheim by Flammer in 1859. *Werke.*

Gedichte von Wilhelm Waiblinger, hrsg. von Eduard Mörike. Hamburg, Georg Heubel, 1844. *Gedichte.*

Bilder aus Neapel und Sicilien, hrsg. von Eduard Grisebach. Leipzig, Richard Eckstein, 1879. *Bilder.*

Die Britten in Rom, hrsg. von Edmund Zoller. Leipzig, Reclam, 1880. *Die Britten in Rom.*

Wilhelm Waiblingers Gedichte aus Italien, hrsg. von Eduard Grisebach. Leipzig, Reclam, 1881-1893. 2 v. *Gedichte aus Italien.*

Liebe und Hass, tragédie inédite de Wilhelm Waiblinger. Berlin, B. Behr, [1913?] (Paris "thèse complémentaire" of André Fauconnet.) *Liebe und Hass* (1913).

Liebe und Hass, hrsg. von André Fauconnet. Berlin, B. Behr, 1914. ("Deutsche Literaturdenkmale des 18. und 19. Jahrhunderts," no. 148.) *Liebe und Hass* (1914).

Der kranke Hölderlin, hrsg. von Paul Friedrich. Leipzig, Xenien-Verlag, n.d. *Der kranke Hölderlin.*

Phaethon, hrsg. von Arthur Schurig. Dresden, Lehmannsche Verlagsbuchhandlung, 1920. *Phaethon.*

Werke, ausgewählt und hrsg. von Paul Friedrich. Berlin, Dom-Verlag, 1922. *Friedrich.*

II. *Other Works Consulted*

Benda, Otto. *Wilhelm Waiblinger.* Prag, Calve, 1905. (Lese- und Redehalle der deutschen Studenten in Prag, *Bericht,* no. 58; "Beilage" I.)

Biese, Alfred. *Das Naturgefühl im Wandel der Zeiten.* Leipzig, Quelle und Meyer, 1926.

Brinckmann, Albert Erich. *Landschaften der deutschen Romantiker.* Berlin, Woldemar Klein, 1935.

Butler, E. M. *The Tyranny of Greece over Germany.* Cambridge, University Press, 1936.

Casanova de Seingalt, Giacomo Girolamo. *Mémoires.* Brussels, J. Rozez, 1876. 6 v.

Fischer, Hermann. *Die schwäbische Literatur im achtzehnten und neunzehnten Jahrhundert.* Tübingen, H. Laupp, 1911.

Fränkel, Ludwig. "Wilhelm Hauff, Wilhelm Waiblinger und H. v. Canitz." Schwäbischer Schillerverein, *Rechenschaftsbericht,* XIX (1915), 90-95.

Frey, Karl. *Wilhelm Waiblinger, sein Leben und seine Werke.* Aarau, Sauerländer, 1904.

Geikie, Archibald. *The Love of Nature among the Romans.* London, Murray, 1912.

---

1. Immediately after each entry in the first part of the bibliography there is the abbreviated title by which the edition concerned is cited in the text. Works in the second part are cited in the text only by the last name of the author.

Glück, Friedrich. *Byronismus bei Waiblinger.* Tübingen diss. Tübingen, H. Laupp, 1920.

Goedecke, Karl. *Grundriss zur Geschichte der deutschen Dichtung.* Dresden, L. Ehlermann, 1884-1951. 13 v. 2nd ed.

Gröner, Otto. *Waiblingers lyrische Gedichte.* Leipzig diss., 1925. Typewritten.

Güntter, Otto, ed. *Hausbuch schwäbischer Erzähler.* Stuttgart, Schwäbischer Schillerverein, 1911.

Hagenmeyer, Gerhard. *Wilhelm Waiblingers Gedichte aus Italien.* Berlin, Emil Ebering, 1930. ("Germanische Studien," no. 92.)

Heinse, Johann Jakob Wilhelm. *Sämmtliche Werke.* Leipzig, Insel Verlag, 1902-1925. 10 v. in 13.

Klenze, Camillo von. *The Interpretation of Italy during the Last Two Centuries.* Chicago, University of Chicago Press, 1907.

Mangère, V. *L'Italie et la romantique.* Paris, Klincksieck, 1902.

Marshall, Roderick. *Italy in English Literature, 1755-1815.* New York, Columbia University Press, 1934.

Meyer, R. M. *Die deutsche Litteratur des neunzehnten Jahrhunderts.* Berlin, Bondi, 1900.

Mörike, Eduard. *Briefe,* hrsg. von Will Vesper. Berlin, Deutsche Bibliothek, n.d.

Porta, G. *Madame de Staël et l'Italie.* Florence, Lapelli, 1902.

Prölss, Johannes. *Deutsch-Capri in Kunst, Leben und Dichtung.* Oldenburg, Schulze, 1901.

Ranke, Leopold von. *Zur eignen Lebensgeschichte,* hrsg. von A. Doré. Leipzig, Reclam, 1890.

Rapp, Moritz. "Wilhelm Waiblinger." *Tübinger Jahrbücher der Gegenwart,* 1847, p. 254-287.

Ruland, Ilse. *Waiblinger in seinen Prosawerken.* Tübingen diss. Stuttgart, Kohlhammer, 1922.

Schultz, Franz. "Goethe und Waiblinger." *Goethe-Jahrbuch,* XXIX (1908), 10-21.

Schumann, Detlev. "The Problem of Generations." *PMLA,* LI (1936), 1180-1208.

Steinitzer, Alfred. *Aus dem unbekannten Italien.* Munich, Piper Verlag, n.d.

Stinde, Julius. *Buchholzens in Italien.* Berlin, Freund und Jaeckel, 1884.

Strich. *Klassik und Romantik oder Vollendung und Unendlichkeit, ein Vergleich.* 3rd ed. Munich, Meyer und Jessen, 1926.

Symonds, John Addington. *The Renaissance in Italy.* New York, Modern Library, 1935. 2 v.

Ubell, H. "Deutsche Gräber in Rom." *Wiener Abendpost,* 1903, no. 43.

Indices

I. Names of Persons[1]

A.

Addison, Joseph, 41, 71, 76.
Adler, Georg Christian, 13, 11.
Aeneas, 51, 52.
Aeschylus, 23.
Alfieri, Vittorio, 32, 33, 35, 37, 96.
Allegri, Antonio, see Coreggio.
Anacreon, 30, 77.
Angelico, Fra Giovanni, da Fiesole, 14, 16, 21, 25, 40, 92.
Archilochus 46.
Ariosto, Lodovico, 14, 30, 32, 34, 40, 54, 66, 84, 85, 86
Arnim, Achim v., 55, 86
August III (elector of Saxony), 13-14
Augustus (Roman emperor), 76.

B.

Baldensperger, J. P. F., 15.
Barbieri, Giovanni Francesco, see Guercino.
Bartoldo, 64.
Bauer, Ludwig, 5, 15, 48, 87.
Beckford, William, 15.
Biese, Alfred, 42.
Blechen, Karl, 42.
Boccaccio, Giovanni, 30, 31, 34, 85.
Börne, Ludwig, 55.
Boiardo, Matteo Maria, 30.
Boisserée Brothers (Sulpice and Melchior), 4, 15, 78.
Bolognesi (painters), 13, 14, 24, 26.
Bourget, Paul, 25.
Brentano, Clemens, 55, 87.
Brinckmann, Albert Erich, 42.
Brockhaus, F. A., 11.
Bruneleschi, Filippo, 24, 84.
Burckhardt, Jakob, 86, 98.
Butler, E. M., 77.
Byron, George Gordon Byron, 3, 9, 16, 29, 41, 43, 44, 70, 73, 76, 80, 82.

C.

Cammarano, Filippo, 34.
Canitz, H. v., 1, 19.
Canova, Antonio, 15, 16, 26, 27, 59.
Caravaggio, Michelangelo Amerighi da, 26.
Casanova de Seingalt, Giacomo Girolamo, 28, 30, 33.
Castiglione, Baldassare, 30.
Catullus, 47, 60.
Cellini, Benvenuto, 24, 28, 81, 84, 86.

Chamisso, Adelbert v., 55.
Chateaubriand, René de, 8, 42, 71.
Chénier, André, 87.
Cimabue, Giovanni, 24.
Clauren, see Heun, Karl Gottlieb Samuel.
Coreggio (i. e., Antonio Allegri), 23.
Cotta, Johann Friedrich, Baron v., 7, 9, 10, 11.

D.

Dannecker, Johann Heinrich v., 4, 15, 78.
Dante, Alighieri, 7, 28, 29, 30, 31, 32, 34, 36.
Dupaty, Charles, 41.

E.

Eichendorff, Joseph v., 14, 15, 20, 42.
Eser, Friedrich, 57, 58, 70.
Euripides, 77.

F.

Fauconnet, André, 1, 2, 82.
Fischer, Hermann, 2, 15.
Flaxman, John, 15.
Fouqué, Friedrich de la Motte-, 7, 20.
Frey, Karl, 2, 16, 22, 27, 30, 50, 57, 77, 87.
Friedrich II (Holy Roman emperor), 22, 23, 88.
Friedrich, Paul, 2, 20, 29, 43, 85, 87.
Fulvius Nobilior, Marcus (Censor), 75.

G.

Geikie, Archibald, 47.
Giotto di Bondone, 24.
Glück, Friedrich, 3, 43.
Goedeke, Karl, 3.
Görres, Joseph, 55, 87, 97.
Goethe, Johann Caspar, 41.
Goethe, Johann Wolfgang v., 1, 8, 14, 15, 16, 22, 25, 26, 28, 29, 41,

---

[1] According to standard rules of library cataloging, entries are under the name by which the individual is best known, with cross references from other names, whether real names or pseudonyms.

42, 43, 47, 49, 54, 58, 64, 70, 72, 78, 81, 82, 95.
Goldoni, Carlo, 32, 33, 34, 35, 96.
Grabbe, Christian Dietrich, 8.
Grahl, August, 59.
Gray, Thomas, 29.
Gregorovius, Ferdinand, 25.
Gregory IX (Pope), 22.
Grimm Brothers, (Jakob and Wilhelm), 35, 55, 63.
Grisebach, Eduard, 1, 50.
Grosse, Julius, 45.
Güntter, Otto, 6.
Guercino, (i.e., Giovanni Francesco Barbieri), 26.

H.
Hagenmeyer, Gerhard, 3, 4.
Hardenberg, Friedrich v., see Novalis.
Haudebourt-Lescot, Antoinette Cécile Hortense, 66.
Hauff, Wilhelm, 86.
Haug, Johann Christoph, 7, 15.
Heim, Philippine, 70.
Heine, Heinrich, 8, 14, 31, 49, 50, 55.
Heinse, Wilhelm, 13, 25, 29, 35, 81, 82, 84.
Herder, Johann Gottfried, 13.
Herodotus, 9.
Heun, Karl Gottlieb Samuel (Clauren), 7.
Heyse, Paul, 45, 98.
Hölderlin, Friedrich, 2, 5, 8, 9, 11, 16, 44, 45, 70, 77.
Hofmannsthal Hugo v., 4.
Hogarth, William, 66.
Hohenstaufen emperors, 22, 88.
Homer, 30, 77, 85.
Horace, 9, 26, 44, 46, 47, 54, 69, 71, 72, 74, 75, 76, 92, 96.
Horn, Franz, 7.
Huggins, William, 84.
Humboldt, Alexander v., 55.
Hunt, Leigh, 82.

I.
Immermann, Karl, 8.
Innocent III (Pope), 22.
Innocent IV (Pope), 22.
Irving, Washington, 80.
Isocrates, 77.

J.
Juvenal, 56, 90.

K.
Klenze, Camillo v., 20, 21, 22, 25, 28, 29, 41, 42, 54, 71, 81.

Kopisch, August, 11, 45.

L.
Lalande, Joseph Jérôme Lefrançais de, 28, 71.
Lamartine, Alphonse Marie Louis de, 42.
Landor, Walter Savage, 82.
Lenau, Nikolaus (i.e., Nikolaus Niembsch, Edler von Strehlenau), 8, 9, 70.
Leo X (Pope), 28.
Lescot, Mlle., see Haudebourt-Lescot, Antoinette Cécile Hortense.
Lessing, Gotthold Ephraim, 1, 13, 82.
Lewis, Mathew Gregory ("Monk"), 5, 82.
Livy, 56.
Louis XIV (king of France), 13, 26.
Lucan, 76.
Lucullus, Lucius Licenius, 47.
Ludwig I (king of Bavaria), 59.
Lysias, 77.

M.
Machiavelli, Niccolò, 30.
Manzoni, Alessandro, 29.
Marcellus, M. Claudius, 79.
Marshall, Roderick, 28, 82, 85.
Martial, 45, 75.
Matthisson, Friedrich v., 15.
Maupassant, Guy de, 25.
Medici, Lorenzo de', 28.
Metastasio, Pietro Antonio Domenico, 32, 33, 34, 35.
Michaelis, Julie, 6, 70.
Michelangelo Buonarroti, 23, 83, 88.
Mörike, Eduard, 1, 2, 5, 6, 20, 29, 43, 48, 72, 87.
Montaigne, Michel Eyquem, 26, 54, 71.
Moritz, Karl Philipp, 8, 13, 20, 81, 82.
Müller, Friedrich (Maler Müller), 8, 87, 97.
Müllner, Adolf, 7.

N.
Nepos, Cornelius, 39.
Nero, 20.
Nesreddin Hoca, 64.
Newton, Isaac, 23.
Novalis (i.e., Friedrich v. Hardenberg), 20, 42, 87.

P.
Penelope, 24.
Persephone, 18.

Perugino, Pietro, 14, 25, 28, 40.
Petrarch, Francesco, 29, 31, 32, 34, 36, 85.
Phidias, 16.
Pichler, Karoline, 7.
Piozzi, Hester Lynch Thrale, 82.
Pius VIII (Pope), 11.
Platen, August, Graf v., 3, 8, 14, 42.
Plato, 77.
Pliny, 28.
Plutarch, 77.
Poussin, Nicolas, 90.
Praxiteles, 16.
Prölss, Johannes, 44.
Pulci, Luigi, 30.

R.
Radcliffe, Anne Ward, 15, 82.
Raphael, 9, 13, 14, 16, 21, 23, 25, 26, 83, 92, 95.
Rapp, Moritz, 2, 8, 44, 89.
Raupach, Ernst, 22.
Reimer, Georg, 10.
Reni, Guido, 13, 24, 26, 90.
Reynolds, Joshua, 82.
Riedesel, J. H., 41.
Romulus, 20.
Roscoe, William, 28.
Rosetti, D. G., 82.
Rossini, Gioachino Antonio, 35.
Rousseau, J.-J., 13, 41.
Rückert, Friedrich, 8.
Ruland, Ilse, 3, 45, 48, 66.
Runge, Philipp Otto, 55.
Ruskin, John, 14.

S.
Saint Francis, 63.
Sarto, Andrea del, 23, 64.
Scheffel, Joseph Viktor v., 45.
Schiller, Friedrich v., 28-29, 37, 82, 87.
Schlegel, August Wilhelm, 8, 29, 30, 34, 82, 95.
Schlegel, Friedrich, 8, 14, 34, 82, 97.
Schluttig, Wilhelm, 11.
Schopenhauer, Arthur, 8.
Schopenhauer, Johanna, 7.
Schultz, Franz, 15.
Schwab, Gustav, 4, 15, 55, 77.
Scopas, 17, 79.
Sgricci, Tommaso, 36, 37, 63, 96.

Shakespeare, William, 23, 29, 33.
Silius Italicus, 71, 76.
Sophocles, 30, 77.
Spina, Francesco, 23, 38, 48, 49.
Spon, Jacob, 13.
Staël-Holstein, Anne Louise Germaine (Necker), baronne de, 8, 14, 29, 35, 38, 95, 96.
Steinitzer, Alfred, 54.
Stinde, Julius, 44.
Strich, Fritz, 8.
Symonds, J. A., 82, 83, 86.

T.
Taddei, Rosa, 35-37, 63, 96.
Tasso, Torquato, 32, 36, 63, 85.
Tenerani, Pietro, 67.
Thorwaldsen, Albert v., 15, 16.
Thucydides, 9.
Tieck, Ludwig, 82.
Timoleon, 73, 79, 80.
Titian, 23, 84.

U.
Uhland, Ludwig, 55.

V.
Van der Velde, 7.
Vasari, Giorgio, 84.
Virgil, 7, 32, 71, 72, 80, 85, 96.
Vitruvius, 28.
Vogelweide, Walther von der, see Walther von der Vogelweide.
Voltaire, F. M. A. de, 87.
Vulpius, Christian August, 5.

W.
Wackenroder, Wilhelm Heinrich, 14.
Wagner, Richard, 36.
Wagner, Theodor, 5, 19.
Walpole, Horace, 71, 82.
Walther von der Vogelweide, 22.
Watteau, Jean Antoine, 41.
Werner, Zacharias, 70, 87, 97.
Winckelmann, Johann Joachim, 13, 22, 28, 41, 49, 71, 78, 95.
Winkler, Karl Gottfried Theodor, 11.

X.
Xenophon, 77.

Z.
Zeno, Apostolo, 33.

II. Names of Places, Buildings, and Works of Art.[1]

A.
Abruzzi, 44, 50, 52.
Aequa Mountains, 50, 51.
Agrigentum, *see* Girgenti.
Alban Hills, 59, 63, 73.
Albano, 59, 65, 89.
Albano, Lago, *see* Lago Albano.
Anagni, 51.
Anio (river), 46.
Apennines, 41, 47, 51, 52.
Apollo de Belvedere, 17.
Appian Way, 52, 96.
Arezzo, 37.
Ariccia, 46.

B.
Bandusian Fountain, 46, 47, 74, 96.
Bellinzona, 5.
Benevento, 42, 52.
Bern, 9.
Blue Grotto, 49.
Borghese, Villa, *see* Villa Borghese.
Brera (art collection, Milan), 5.
Brindisi, 56.

C.
Café Greco (Rome), 62.
Caffè degli Specchi (Rome), 38.
Campania, 41.
Campo Vaccino (Forum Roman-um), 20, 43, 96.
Capranica, 50.
Capri, 44, 45.
Cavallo, Monte, *see* Monte Cavallo.
Cavo, Monte, *see* Monte Cavo.
Cenis, Mont, *see* Mont Cenis.
Cestius, Pyramid of, *see* Pyramid of Cestius.
Civitella, 50, 61, 92.
Colonna, Piazza, *see* Piazza Colon-na.
Colosseum, 20, 48.
Como, Lago, *see* Lago Como.
Cori, 75.

D.
Delphi, 72.
Dresden Staatsgalerie, 14.

E.
Egeria, spring of (Nemi), 45.

F.
Florence, 9, 17, 27, 28, 31, 79.
Forum Romanum, *see* Campo Vac-cino.
Frascati (and ancient Tusculum), 46, 59, 60.
Fucino, Lago, *see* Lago Fucino.

G.
Garda, Lago di, *see* Lago di Garda.
Geneva, 9.
Genoa, 9.
Genzano, 54, 59, 65, 66, 73, 85, 86.
Gianicolo, 63.
Girgenti, (ancient Agrigentum), 18, 21, 51, 53, 79, 80.

H.
Heilbronn, 4.

J.
Jupiter Stator (temple of), 76.

L.
Lago Albano, 43, 44, 45, 52, 73.
Lago Como, 5.
Lago di Garda, 47.
Lago Fucino, 47.
Lago Nemi, 65, 71.
Latium, 44, 45, 50, 56, 80, 88.
Lavinium, 51, 52.
Licenza, 92.
Liguria, 52.
Lombardy, 41, 52.
London, 7.

M.
Maleventum, *see* Benevento.
Milan, 5.
Minerva Medica (temple of), 49.
Monreale, 22.
Mont Cenis, 9.
Monte Cavallo, 16.
Monte Cavo, 52.
Monte San Vito, 50.
Locarno, 5.
Montefiascone, 9.
Monte Testaccio (Rome), 57.

N.
Naples, 10, 11, 34, 42, 49, 52, 54, 56, 67, 71.
Nemi, 44, 45, 47.
Nemi, Lago, *see* Lago Nemi.
Neptune, grotto of (Tivoli), 47.

O.
Olevano, 36, 39, 47, 48, 50, 51, 55, 59, 62, 89.
Ortygia (Delos), 18.
Ostia, 97.

---

[1] Classical localities are entered under modern names (if any), with cross references from the ancient names.

P.

Palermo, 22.
Palestrina (ancient Praeneste), 46, 61, 89.
Paris, 50.
Parthenope, 52.
Piazza Colonna (Rome), 38.
Piazza del Quirinale (Rome), 16.
Piazza Rusticucci (Rome), 56.
Piedmont, 9.
Pisa, 9, 27.
Pitti Gallery (Florence), 9.
Pompeii, 74-75, 76.
Pontine Marshes, 46, 52.
Ponza Islands, 52.
Praeneste, see Palestrina.
Pyramid of Cestius, 11.

Q.

Quirinale, Piazza del, see Piazza del Quirinale.

R.

Reutlingen, 4.
Rome, 5, 9, 10, 11, 13, 15, 16, 18, 20, 27, 33, 36, 38, 43, 44, 45, 48, 52, 54, 55, 58, 62, 63, 65, 68, 69, 71, 72, 74, 76, 77, 79, 80, 87, 88, 92, 95, 97, 98.
Rusticucci, Piazza, see Piazza Rusticucci.

S.

Sabine Hills, 9, 10, 36, 50, 59, 88.
Saint Gotthard, 5, 6.
Saint Peter's Cathedral (Rome), 56, 89, 90, 91.
San Carlino Theatre (Naples), 34.
San Vito, Monte, see Monte San Vito.
Sasso di Dante (Florence), 31.
Scipios (Mausoleum of the), 19, 27, 45, 75.
Segni, 51.
Sicily, 11, 17, 21, 22, 23, 41, 44, 46, 73, 78, 79, 96.

Siena, 9.
Sirmio, 47.
Soracte, 9.
Sorrento, 44, 45, 51.
Spezia, 42.
Stuttgart, 2, 3, 4, 7, 11, 15, 78.
Subiaco, 52, 59.
Susa, 9.
Syracuse, 21, 52, 79.

T.

Terracina, 65.
Testaccio, Monte, see Monte Testaccio.
Thermae of Titus, 48.
Timoleon (Villa of), 73, 80.
Tivoli (ancient Tibur), 41, 44, 46, 47, 51, 72.
Tocca di Cavi, 50.
Torre dell' Annunziata, 92.
Trapani, 44.
Troy, 52.
Tübingen, 2, 3, 5, 6, 7, 11, 44, 87.
Tuscany, 9.
Tusculum, see Frascati.
Tyrrhenian Sea, 52.

U.

Uffizi Gallery (Florence), 9.
Urach, 4.

V.

Venice, 6, 33, 42.
Venus of Milo, 17, 78.
Venus of the Capitol, 78.
Venus of the Medici, 79.
Verona, 6.
Vesuvius, 92.
Villa Borghese (Rome), 57.
Villa Giustiniani, 49.
Vito, Monte San, see Monte San Vito.

Z.

Zürich, 9.

CPSIA information can be obtained
at www.ICGtesting.com
Printed in the USA
LVHW031315300621
691479LV00006B/626